A MODERN FORM OF SLAVERY

Trafficking of Burmese Women and Girls into Brothels in Thailand

Asia Watch
and
The Women's Rights Project

Human Rights Watch
New York • Washington • Los Angeles • London

Library of Congress Catalog Card Number: 93-81036
ISBN 1-56432-107-X

Cover illustration by Pamela Blotner for Human Rights Watch. Drawing based on a photograph of Burmese women awaiting clients in a Thai brothel.

HUMAN RIGHTS WATCH

Human Rights Watch conducts regular, systematic investigations of human rights abuses in some seventy countries around the world. It addresses the human rights practices of governments of all political stripes, of all geopolitical alignments, and of all ethnic and religious persuasions. In internal wars it documents violations by both governments and rebel groups. Human Rights Watch defends freedom of thought and expression, due process and equal protection of the law; it documents and denounces murders, disappearances, torture, arbitrary imprisonment, exile, censorship and other abuses of internationally recognized human rights.

Human Rights Watch began in 1978 with the founding of its Helsinki division. Today, it includes five divisions covering Africa, the Americas, Asia, the Middle East, as well as the signatories of the Helsinki accords. It also includes four collaborative projects on Arms, Free Expression, Prisoners' Rights, and Womens Rights. It now maintains offices in New York, Washington, Los Angeles, London, Moscow, Belgrade, Zagreb and Hong Kong. Human Rights Watch is an independent, nongovernmental organization, supported by contributions from private individuals and foundations. It accepts no government funds, directly or indirectly.

The board includes Robert L. Bernstein, chair; Adrian W. DeWind, vice chair; Roland Algrant, Lisa Anderson, Peter D. Bell, Alice L. Brown, William Carmichael, Dorothy Cullman, Irene Diamond, Jonathan Fanton, Alan Finberg, Jack Greenberg, Alice H. Henkin, Stephen L. Kass, Marina Pinto Kaufman, Alexander MacGregor, Peter Osnos, Kathleen Peratis, Bruce Rabb, Orville Schell, Gary G. Sick, and Malcolm Smith.

The staff includes Kenneth Roth, executive director; Holly J. Burkhalter, Washington director; Gara LaMarche, associate director; Susan Osnos, press director; Ellen Lutz, California director; Jemera Rone, counsel; Richard Dicker, associate counsel; Stephanie Steele, operations director; Michal Longfelder, development director; Rachel Weintraub, special events director; Allyson Collins, research associate; and Ham Fish, senior advisor.

The regional directors of Human Rights Watch are Abdullahi An-Na'im, Africa; Juan E. Méndez, Americas; Sidney Jones, Asia; Jeri Laber, Helsinki; and Andrew Whitley, Middle East. The project directors are Kenneth Anderson, Arms; Gara LaMarche, Free Expression; Joanna Weschler, Prisoners' Rights; and Dorothy Q. Thomas, Women's Rights.

Addresses for Human Rights Watch

485 Fifth Avenue
New York, NY 10017-6104
Tel: (212) 972-8400
Fax: (212) 972-0905
email: hrwatchnyc@igc.apc.org

1522 K Street, N.W., #910
Washington, DC 20005
Tel: (202) 371-6592
Fax: (202) 371-0124
email: hrwatchdc@igc.apc.org

10951 West Pico Blvd., #203
Los Angeles, CA 90064
Tel: (310) 475-3070
Fax: (310) 475-5613
email: hrwatchla@igc.apc.org

90 Borough High Street
London, UK SE1 1LL
Tel: (071) 378-8008
Fax: (071) 378-8029
email: hrwatchuk@gn.org

TABLE OF CONTENTS

ACKNOWLEDGEMENTS vii
I. INTRODUCTION 1
II. BACKGROUND 10
    A. POLITICAL AND ECONOMIC FACTORS 10
        International Response and Thai-Burmese
        Relations (12); Economic Factors (15);
        Immigration (17)
    B. RELEVANT NATIONAL AND INTERNATIONAL
        LAW 20
        The 1928 Anti-Trafficking Act (21); 1960
        Criminalization of Prostitution (22); The
        Entertainment Places Act and the Penal Code
        (24)
III. THREE PORTRAITS 38
    "LIN LIN" 38
    "NYI NYI" 41
    "SWE SWE" 43
IV. TRAFFICKING IN WOMEN AND GIRLS 45
    A. RECRUITMENT 45
        The Promises (46); The Money (48); Sexual
        Abuse in the Course of Recruitment (49);
        Moving From Brothel to Brothel (51); Ranong
        (52)
    B. THE BROTHEL 53
        Debt Bondage (53); Illegal Confinement (59);
        Rape and Other Forms of Sexual and Physical
        Abuse (62); Working Conditions (67); Health
        Care, Birth Control and AIDS (68)
V. THE THAI GOVERNMENT'S ROLE 75
    A. OFFICIAL INVOLVEMENT IN TRAFFICKING: A
        PATTERN OF IMPUNITY 75
        The Songkhla Murder (80)
    B. NON-ARREST OF TRAFFICKERS, PIMPS,
        PROCURERS, BROTHEL OWNERS AND
        CLIENTS 82
    C. DISCRIMINATORY AND ARBITRARY ARREST
        OF TRAFFICKING VICTIMS 84
    D. VIOLATIONS OF DUE PROCESS 86
    E. PROLONGED DETENTION, SUMMARY TRIALS

AND CUSTODIAL ABUSE 89
Local Jails (91); Immigration Detention Center
(IDC) (91); Emergency Shelters (100)
F. DEPORTATION 101
Summary Deportation: The Thai Side (101);
Deportation from Ranong (102); Deportation
From Kanchanaburi (104); Discreet Returns
over the Border (110); Summary Deportation:
The Burmese Side (111)
G. THE NON-PENAL ALTERNATIVE: OFFICIAL
REPATRIATION 114
VI. NON-GOVERNMENTAL ORGANIZATIONS (NGOs) 120
NGOS IN THAILAND 120
NGOS IN BURMA............................. 124
VII. CAPTIVE PARTNERS: FORCED PROSTITUTION AND
HIV/AIDS 125
A. ABUSES THAT LEAD TO HIV INFECTION 126
B. THAI GOVERNMENT ACCOUNTABILITY 128
C. ABUSES ARISING FROM PERCEIVED OR
ACTUAL HIV STATUS 132
Mandatory HIV testing (132); Testing in the
brothels (135); Testing in official custody (137);
Testing at the Temporary Shelters (138);
Breach of Medical Confidentiality (139);
Discrimination (142)
D. WITHHOLDING INFORMATION ABOUT
HIV/AIDS 144
E. TREATMENT ON RETURN TO BURMA 146
VIII. INTERNATIONAL RESPONSE 148
U.S. POLICY AND TRAFFICKING 148
OTHER COUNTRIES 149
HIV AND AIDS 149
UNITED NATIONS AGENCIES 151
IX. CONCLUSIONS AND RECOMMENDATIONS 152

ACKNOWLEDGEMENTS

Research for this report was undertaken by an Asia Watch staff member who must remain anonymous, with additional research by the Women's Rights Project. It was written by the Asia Watch researcher together with Dorothy Q. Thomas, director of the Women's Rights Project and Sidney Jones, executive director of Asia Watch. Sarah Lai of the Women's Rights Project researched and wrote Chapter VII. The report was edited by Thomas and Jones. We would like to acknowledge with gratitude and admiration the help of many people in Thailand, both Thai and Burmese, who cannot be named.

I. INTRODUCTION

"Lin Lin" was thirteen years old when she was recruited by an agent for work in Thailand. Her father took $480 from the agent with the understanding that his daughter would pay the loan back out of her earnings. The agent took "Lin Lin" to Bangkok, and three days later she was taken to the Ran Dee Prom brothel. "Lin Lin" did not know what was going on until a man came into her room and started touching her breasts and body and then forced her to have sex. For the next two years, "Lin Lin" worked in various parts of Thailand in four different brothels, all but one owned by the same family. The owners told her she would have to keep prostituting herself until she paid off her father's debt. Her clients, who often included police, paid the owner $4 each time. If she refused a client's demands, she was slapped and threatened by the owner. She worked every day except for the two days off each month she was allowed for her menstrual period. Once she had to borrow money to pay for medicine to treat a painful vaginal infection. This amount was added to her debt. On January 18, 1993 the Crime Suppression Division of the Thai police raided the brothel in which "Lin Lin" worked, and she was taken to a shelter run by a local non-governmental organization. She was fifteen years old, had spent over two years of her young life in compulsory prostitution, and tested positive for the human immunodeficiency virus or HIV.

"Lin Lin" is just one of thousands of Burmese women and girls who have been trafficked and sold into what amounts to female sexual slavery in Thailand. In the last two years, Thai NGOs estimate that at a minimum, some twenty thousand Burmese women and girls are suffering Lee's fate, or worse, and that ten thousand new recruits come in every year. They are moved from one brothel to another as the demand for new faces dictates, and often end up being sent back to Burma after a year or two to recruit their own successors.

These Burmese women and girls are only a fraction of the estimated 800,000 to two million prostitutes currently working in Thailand. We focus this report on the Burmese trafficking victims because of the range of violations of internationally-recognized human rights that they suffer, from debt bondage to arbitrary detention, and because government officials, particularly form Thailand, are complicit in these violations both by direct involvement in the brothels and by failing to enforce Thailand's obligations under both national and international law.

The Women's Rights Project and Asia Watch, both divisions of

1

Human Rights Watch, traveled to Thailand to investigate the trafficking of Burmese women and girls into prostitution and to assess the responsibility of the Thai government for this problem. We made three trips to Thailand: in September 1992 for three weeks, in January and February 1993 for three weeks, and July 1993 for one week. On the first trip, an Asia Watch staff member fluent in Thai was accompanied by a consultant who was fluent in Burmese and Shan. Together they interviewed thirty Burmese women and girls in depth, most from remote rural villages in Shan state, most from peasant or agricultural laborer backgrounds. They ranged in age from twelve to twenty-two, although the average age was seventeen. All but one had been lured to Thailand by the prospect of improving their economic situation. Only four knew they would be working as prostitutes, and even those four had no idea of what the actual work would be like.

Most of our interviews took place at emergency shelters for trafficking victims run by non-governmental organizations (NGOs) in Chiangmai and Bangkok. We were also able to speak with women and girls detained at the Immigration Detention Center in Bangkok. In the course of the three visits, we conducted interviews along the Thai-Burmese border in Mae Sai, Three Pagodas Pass and Ranong. In addition to our own interviews, we had access to other primary source material, including the transcripts of twenty-one interviews with Burmese women conducted by an NGO in Chiangmai in October 1992. We interviewed officials in Mae Sai, Chiangmai and Bangkok, including Police Colonel Surasak Suttharom, the deputy commander of the Crime Suppression Division of the Thai police, and Dr. Saisuree Chutikul, a member of the Thai cabinet in 1992 and, after the September 1992 elections, an adviser to the new Chuan administration. Finally, we consulted with academic specialists such as Dr. Vicharn Vithayasai of the Faculty of Medicine at Chiangmai University.

In the interviews with the women and girls, we realized that simple questions and answers masked a much more complex reality. For example, many of the girls, when asked if they knew they would be working in prostitution before they came to Thailand, said, "Yes." But when we asked what they understood prostitution to be, we would get responses such as "wearing Western clothes in a restaurant." Likewise, when asked if they were able to leave the brothels freely, many initially said, "Yes." But when asked if in fact they had ever tried to leave, almost all said they had not dared to do so because they had no money or because they feared being arrested or sold to another brothel. When we asked if they could refuse clients, again, the answer was almost unanimously, "Yes." Yet asked to give specific examples, most could not, and it turned out that refusal was almost unheard of because the women and girls feared repercussions from the brothel owner and pimps. Only slowly did the reality of recruitment and life in the brothels emerge.

Throughout this report, we draw on material from the original thirty interviews for examples, using Burmese pseudonyms for the real names of the victims.

THE NATURE OF THE ABUSE

The trafficking of Burmese women and girls into Thailand is appalling in its efficiency and ruthlessness. Driven by the desire to maximize profit and by the fear of HIV/AIDS, agents acting on behalf of brothel owners infiltrate ever more remote areas of Burma seeking unsuspecting recruits. Virgin girls are particularly sought after because they bring a higher price and pose less of a threat of exposure to sexually transmitted disease. The agents promise the women and girls jobs as waitresses or dishwashers, with good pay and new clothes. Family members or friends typically accompany the women and girls to the Thai border, where they receive a payment ranging from 10,000 baht ($400) to 20,000 baht ($800) from someone associated with the brothel. This payment becomes the debt, usually doubled with interest, that the women and girls must work to pay off, not by waitressing or dishwashing, but through sexual servitude.

Once the women and girls are confined in the Thai brothels, escape is virtually impossible. Any Burmese woman or girl who steps outside the brothel risks physical punishment, retribution against her parents or relatives for defaulting on her debt and/or arrest as an illegal immigrant -- by the same police who are often the brothel owner's best clients. The worst brothels in the southern Thai town of Ranong are surrounded by electrified barbed wire and armed guards.

The women and girls face a wide range of abuse, including debt bondage; illegal confinement; forced labor; rape; physical abuse; exposure to HIV/AIDS; and in some cases, murder. Initially, young girls like "Lin Lin" are kept in what is known as the *hong bud boree sut*, literally "the room to unveil virgins." Later they are moved to the *hong du*, or "selection" room, where they are displayed in windowed enclosures wearing numbers. The sex occurs in small cubicles where the women and girls also live and where the bed is often little more than a concrete bunk.

Working conditions are inhumane. The women and girls work ten to eighteen hours a day, about twenty-five days a month. They average between five and fifteen clients a day. Health care and birth control education are minimal. In some instances, pregnant women are forced either to abort illegally or to continue to service clients well into their pregnancies. Many of the girls and women are brought to Thailand as virgins; most return with HIV. Fifty to seventy percent of the women and girls we interviewed were HIV positive.

Their HIV/AIDS positive status frequently results in further abuse, often while the women and girls are in official custody. We found that many of the women and girls were tested for HIV, without their informed consent and sometimes without even their knowledge, not only by brothel owners but also by public health officials. Those who were aware of having been tested were often denied the results of their own tests, even as outcomes were made available to brothel owners, immigration officials and others. This breach of medical confidentiality not only violates Thai law and the women and girls' fundamental rights to privacy, but may have dangerous consequences for the treatment of these women and girls on return to Burma.

The government of Thailand recognizes that trafficking in women and girls is widespread and, particularly in the last two years under Prime Ministers Anand Panyarachun and Chuan Leekpai, has undertaken some limited reforms, both legal and institutional, which are described more fully in the next chapter. In November 1992, for example, Prime Minister Chuan pledged to crack down on child and forced prostitution. A number of high-profile raids on illegal brothels followed. But more than a year later, the trafficking of Burmese women and girls continues virtually unchecked and according to some local activists, is on the increase. Despite clear evidence of direct official involvement in every stage of the trafficking process, not a single Thai officer, to our knowledge, has been investigated or prosecuted except in one highly publicized case of murder.[1] For the most part, agents, pimps, brothel owners and clients have also been exempt from punishment. In fact, the main victims of the Chuan administration's crackdown on forced and child prostitution appear to be the victims of such abuse themselves, whom police routinely subject to discriminatory and wrongful arrest and summary deportation.

Legal safeguards are either lacking or poorly enforced. The Thai government has yet to ratify or accede to most of the international instruments relevant to trafficking in women and girls, such as the International Covenant on Civil and Political Rights and the 1949 Convention for the Suppression of the Traffic in Persons and of the Exploitation of the Prostitution of Others. Nonetheless, under customary international law, Thailand has an obligation to eliminate slavery and all slave-related practices, including trafficking and debt bondage. In addition, Thailand's obligations under the Convention to Eliminate All Forms of Discrimination Against Women (CEDAW), to which Thailand acceded in 1985, further requires the government to eliminate discrimination against women and to take all appropriate measures to suppress trafficking in women and girls. Thai national law also prohibits discrimination on the basis of sex, trafficking in women and girls, prostitution, procurement for prostitution, debt bondage, illegal confinement and rape and physical assault. Yet, despite these clear international and national obligations and prohibitions, the Thai government has consistently failed to punish offenders and instead has routinely arrested female victims as illegal immigrants or prostitutes or both and summarily deported them back to Burma.

This discriminatory pattern of arrest is made all that much more egregious by the fact that under both national and international law, the women and girls should never have been arrested in the first instance. Under international anti-trafficking norms and Thai domestic law, trafficking victims are clearly exempt from fines or imprisonment and guaranteed safe repatriation back to their country of origin. The Thai

---

[1] Police were prosecuted in the highly-publicized murder of a prostitute in Songkhla in November 1992 and evidence of police links to the brothel owner was established. But we know of no member of the police or border patrol prosecuted for complicity in the recruiting or transport of Burmese women and girls into Thailand, for rape or sexual abuse or for complicity in forcing the women and girls to work as bonded labor.

government's attitude toward Burmese trafficking victims contrasts with its efforts on behalf of Thai women trafficked into Japan and subsequently arrested as illegal immigrants. When the Japanese government indicated in July 1993 that it planned to crack down on illegal immigrants in August, Thai officials urged Japan to "waive the use of jail as a punishment for all Thais facing arrest and secure reliable measures to protect Thai women from harassment by their gangster bosses."[2] Thailand also urged Japan to pay all repatriation costs and to form a "repatriation committee" to arrange the workers' safe return to Thailand.

Not only are the arrests of the Burmese women and girls in Thailand discriminatory, but they are carried out with little respect for the women's and girls' fundamental rights to due process. They often are conducted without warrant, and the women and girls are subsequently held, often for long periods, without charge or trial. Where legal procedures do occur, they are routinely conducted in Thai, a language that the women and girls for the most part cannot understand. In the course of their detention and deportation the Burmese women and girls often experience horrific prison conditions and routine custodial abuse.

The process of deporting Burmese women and girls to the border involves a new round of extortion and sexual abuse as Thai officials exploit the pervasive fear these women and girls have of being handed back to Burmese authorities. A Thai policeman in a border detention center may offer to bring a girl back to Bangkok if she will sleep with him or simply take a woman detainee by force with little fear of repercussion. Getting down from a bus or truck at the deportation site, without money and terrified of being arrested once they cross the border, Burmese women and girls find themselves surrounded by brothel agents offering them jobs -- and the cycle begins again. The deportation process in many cases thus becomes a revolving door back to the brothels.

Information about what happens to the women and girls once they return to Burma is not readily available. Under the State Law and Order Restoration Council or SLORC, Burma has acquired one of the worst human rights records in Asia. No domestic human rights organizations exist, and no international non-governmental human rights organizations are allowed access to the country. Giving information to

---

[2] *Kyodo News Service*, July 27, 1993, in *Foreign Broadcast Information Service* FBIS-EAS-93-143, July 28, 1993, p.78.

such organizations or to journalists is grounds for arrest, and surreptitious efforts to make inquiries about returnees can put the latter in serious jeopardy.

This much is clear, even when the women and girls have finally returned to their country of origin: after months and in some cases years of sexual enslavement, they still are not safe from abuse. Rather than returning them safely to their families, the Burmese government often arrests the women and girls for having left the country illegally or engaged in prostitution, both of which constitute offenses under Burmese law.

THE NEED FOR ACTION

At one point, during the administration of Prime Minister Anand Panyarachun in 1992, the Thai authorities began to recognize that no justification, legal or otherwise, existed for arresting and deporting the Burmese women and girls and subjecting them to near certain abuse on return to Burma. Working with Burmese authorities, then Minister Saisuree Chutikul arranged an official repatriation of ninety-five Burmese women and girls.

This unprecedented official repatriation process was plagued with problems, most notably the lengthy remand of the women and girls without charge or trial to penal reform institutions pending their repatriation; official Thai complicity in discrimination against non-ethnic Burman women and girls; and lack of follow-up once the official repatriation was complete. Nonetheless, it marked an important effort by Thai and Burmese authorities to craft an approach to trafficking victims responsive to their plight and consistent with international law. Unfortunately, rather than further refining this approach, the Thai government appears to have abandoned it entirely.

But Thailand has the greatest responsibility for protecting the women and girls whose human rights are violated on its territory, with the knowledge and complicity of its officials. The Thai government must ensure that Burmese women and girls trafficked into prostitution and forced into a situation tantamount to sexual slavery are not punished and that all those complicit in the trafficking are prosecuted and punished to the fullest extent of the law. To this end, Thailand should expand legal protection for the Burmese women and girls through accession to or ratification of relevant international standards and exempt them (and all others forced or lured into prostitution) from punishment under domestic laws relating to immigration and prostitution. The Thai government must also discontinue summary deportation and institute non-penal alternatives to assist the women and girls to leave the brothels and return safely to Burma. It should also actively investigate and prosecute all those involved in trafficking and brothel operations, with particular attention to its own police force and government officials who collaborate with or profit from those operations.

Many observers, despairing that the Thai government will meet its international obligations to protect trafficking victims, have advocated a greater role for Thai non-governmental organizations. These NGOs have played a vital role in raising the visibility of the problem of trafficking and its attendant abuses, advocating important legal reforms and providing services to the tiny fraction of trafficking victims who have the good fortune to end up in NGO-run shelters. But NGOs cannot and should not be expected to shoulder responsibilities that the Thai government has shirked. They are woefully underfunded and understaffed. Even unlimited resources to help women "rescued" from the brothels, in the absence of the government's political will to punish the traffickers, would only increase the demand for services without in any way addressing the root cause of the problem.

The international community can help. For well over a century and at a minimum since the Slavery Convention of 1926, the international community has condemned slavery and slavery-related practices and worked toward the abolition of such abuse wherever it occurs. Female sexual slavery has also been clearly condemned, most notably in the 1949 Convention on the Suppression of Traffic in Persons and the Exploitation of the Prostitution of Others. But unlike other slavery-related practices, female sexual slavery routinely escapes effective national and international sanction. Often it is mischaracterized as prostitution or is dismissed as an abuse perpetrated by private individuals for which states have no responsibility under international human rights law. As a result, at the close of the twentieth century, female sexual slavery, which involves the transport and sale of women into forced prostitution, servile forms of marriage and other forms of compulsory sexual service is widely and increasingly practiced, not only in Thailand but also in many other parts of the world.

The international community must step up pressure not only on the Thai government, to meet its international obligations, but the

Burmese government as well. Just as the Thai police raid the same brothels they patronize and arrest women as illegal immigrants whom they may have hired the night before, Burmese officials arrest deported women and girls for illegal departure whose recruitment to Thailand they may have facilitated by taking bribes from brothel agents. It is incumbent on the Burmese government to investigate and prosecute those involved in trafficking on the Burmese side of the border. Just as important for the safety and well-being of the women and girls, however, is pressure on SLORC to allow regular access to Burmese villages and detention centers by international human rights and humanitarian organizations.

None of the measures needed to stop trafficking and related abuses will take place without concerted international pressure because there is too much money to be made from the practice. This pressure must come from countries like the United States and Japan which have close relations with Thailand; from the countries of the Association of Southeast Asian Nations (ASEAN) which also have an interest in ending trafficking; from China, whose women are also being sold into Thai brothels and from international organizations such as the United Nations.

It is long past time for the international community to realize that women and children in many parts of the world are being sold on the international market like any other commodity. No justification whatsoever exist for presuming the consent of the victims to such treatment or for failing to hold their abusers accountable.

II. BACKGROUND

A. POLITICAL AND ECONOMIC FACTORS

The number of Burmese women recruited to work in Thai brothels has soared in recent years as an indirect consequence of repression in Burma (Myanmar)[3] by the ruling State Law and Order Restoration Council (SLORC) and of improved economic relations between Burma and Thailand.

Human rights violations, war and ethnic discrimination had displaced hundreds of thousands of Burmese between 1962, when Burmese strongman Ne Win took power in a coup, and September 1988, when mass street protests against the government in Rangoon and elsewhere led to a crackdown by the Burmese military. An estimated 3,000 people were killed, and thousands fled the country. Mounting domestic and international pressure led the government to hold elections in May 1990 that the opposition, led by Nobel Peace Prize laureate Aung San Suu Kyi, won handily. The military, however, refused to hand over power and tightened its control, arresting thousands and forcing thousands more to flee into Thailand or join forces with several armed ethnic insurgencies operating along the Thai and Chinese borders.

Despite some cosmetic changes and some widely publicized prisoner releases (not including Aung San Suu Kyi who remains under house arrest), little has changed since then.[4] Late 1991 saw the beginning of one of the most intensive dry-season offensives ever mounted by Burmese troops against minorities living along the borders of Thailand, China and Bangladesh. The military operations appeared to be directed not only at ending armed insurgencies which had been active along the borders since the 1940s, but also at promoting an ethnically

---

[3] Burma was officially renamed Myanmar on June 18, 1990 by the ruling military government called State Law and Order Restoration Council (SLORC). While the new name has been adopted by the United Nations, many Burmese understand the use of "Myanmar" as a de facto recognition of SLORC's authority and prefer to use "Burma."

[4] Asia Watch, *Burma: Changes in Burma?* Vol.4, No.24 (New York: Human Rights Watch, September 6, 1992)

Burman, Buddhist culture.[5]

By the end of 1993, fighting was at its lowest level in years, and SLORC was engaged in a concerted effort to negotiate cease-fires with different minority groups. But throughout 1992 and 1993, the Burmese army continued to employ the "four cuts" strategy, designed to cut off the rebel armies' food, funds, intelligence and recruits. This meant forced removals of entire villages along the Burmese side of the Thai border and the transformation of populated areas into no-man's-lands, leading in turn to a mass exodus of villagers into Thailand. Thai officials in June 1993 estimated that 1,200 Burmese a month were coming across the border from the war-torn Mon and Karen states, because of unemployment, commodity scarcities and fear of being conscripted as porters by the Burmese military.[6] Conclusion

*Since 1990, the United Nations Commission on Human Rights has undertaken to investigate the human rights situation in Burma, first through a confidential procedure and in 1992 and 1993 through the appointment of a Special Rapporteur, Professor Yozo Yokota of Japan. In February 1993, Professor Yokota presented his first report to the Commission based on a visit the previous December, noting a pattern of systematic government abuse including torture, arbitrary executions and disappearances.[7] He returned to Burma in November 1993 and submitted a preliminary report to the U.N. General Assembly at the end of November, noting a few developments which "may lead to improvements" in the human rights situation but emphasizing the "many serious restrictions and grave violations of human rights and fundamental freedoms continuing in Myanmar."[8] These restrictions included at least

---

[5] Asia Watch, *Burma: Rape, Forced Labor and Religious Persecution in Northern Arakan* Vol.4, No.13 (New York: Human Rights Watch, May 7, 1992)

[6] "Flow of Illegal Immigrants Called Problem," *The Nation*, June 13, 1993.

[7] *Report on the Situation of Human Rights in Myanmar*, prepared by Yozo Yokota, Special Rapporteur of the Commission on Human Rights, February 17, 1993, E/CN.4/1993/37.

[8] Introductory Statement by the Special Rapporteur on the Situation of Human Rights in Myanmar, Professor Yozo Yokota, to the Third Committee, 24 November 1993.

500 political leaders still in detention, including Aung San Suu Kyi whom Professor Yokota was not permitted to visit; widespread violations of the right to life and freedom from torture and slavery; and ongoing problems with forced labor and forced relocation. General restrictions also continued on the freedoms of expression, association and assembly.

International Response and Thai-Burmese Relations

Most donor countries responded to the 1988 crackdown and subsequent human rights abuses in Burma with economic sanctions and withdrawal of foreign aid.[9] SLORC, desperate for foreign exchange, turned to Thailand at the end of 1988, offering a range of economic concessions for fishing, logging, gem mining and exploitation of gas and other natural resources. The beneficiaries were often highly placed Thai officials with the ability to influence foreign policy. When he was Supreme Commander and Army Chief of the Thai army, General Chavalit Yongchaiyudh secured profitable logging and fishing concessions after an official visit to Rangoon on December 14, 1988. In January and February 1989, he deported over 300 Burmese student refugees back to Burma in an apparent effort to keep his relations with the SLORC leadership intact.[10]

Such economic links led to official openings of new border crossings along the Thai-Burmese border. In the past, the crossings operated on an informal basis and were poorly regulated by both governments. The formalization has allowed both Thai and Burmese citizens to more easily cross their common border.[11] For example, in April 1993, the Thai Cabinet approved a proposal from the Ministry of the Interior to open fourteen temporary border crossings to facilitate the

---

[9] Japan, Burma's major donor, initially suspended all foreign aid (Official Development Assistance or ODA) after the September 1988 crackdown, but resumed aid for ongoing projects in February 1989.

[10] Asia Watch, *"Abuses Against Burmese Refugees in Thailand,"* Vol.4 No.7 (New York:Human Rights Watch, 1992). See also: "Different Strokes," *Far Eastern Economic Review*, February 23, 1989.

[11] "New Border Checkpoints Open," *Bangkok Post*, October 7, 1992.

importation of logs.[12] An Interior Ministry spokesman said that relevant government agencies would have to ensure that the logs were properly felled and that "the smuggling of war weapons, drug and illegal commodities is not involved in the logging business."[13] Two months later, the Burmese government threatened to end timber and fishing concessions, apparently because of the income they provided to armed rebels from ethnic minority groups operating in and around many of the logging areas.

Nevertheless, cross-border trade appeared to be increasing. Cease-fire and trade agreements between SLORC and minority groups in northern Burma led to the opening up in 1992 of the northeastern corner of the country, facilitating trade with Thailand and China. Both Thailand and Burma began promoting tourism to the Golden Triangle area,[14] and the Thai press reported plans for the construction of a major new road through China, Burma and Thailand. The new road would link Mae Sai on the Thai side with Keng Tung in Burma, an area from which many of the women and girls we interviewed for this report originally came.[15]

The opening of trade and border crossings has facilitated the rise in trafficking of Burmese, men, women and children, with the same routes used to transport people as are used to transport drugs and goods.[16] The most important towns for cross border trade are Mae Sai,

---

[12] "14 Border Crossings to Help Log Import Trade," *The Nation*, April 28, 1993.

[13] Ibid.

[14] The Golden Triangle refers to the area where the borders of Thailand, Burma and Laos meet. This area is renowned for its production and distribution of opium and heroin.

[15] "Thailand-Burma-China Road Link Nearer Reality," *Horizons*, June 1993.

[16] Two Hong Kong Chinese suspected of being major suppliers of drugs to markets in the United States and Canada were arrested in Bangkok on June 26, 1993. They were suspected of smuggling mainland Chinese into Thailand (almost certainly via Burma, as Thailand has no border with China) as well as luring women into prostitution in Malaysia. "Police Arrest Two Foreign Drug Suspects," *Bangkok Post*, June 27, 1993.

in the northwest corner of Thailand, just across the border from the
Burmese town of Taichelek; Mae Sot across from Myawaddy; Three
Pagodas Pass bordering Thailand's Kanchanaburi Province and Burma's
Ye Township; and Ranong, in southern Thailand across from Kawthaung.

The association between improved Thai-Burmese trade relations
and the increasing number of Burmese women in Thai brothels is most
obvious in the southern Thai town of Ranong, where fishing and logging
concessions in Burma have provided the primary source of income since
the 1988 uprisings. According to the *Bangkok Post* of September 13, 1992,
"Ninety-nine percent of all business in Ranong involves border trade with
Burma and/or depends on Burmese labor." The number of brothels in the
town multiplied threefold between 1988 and 1992.[17] The chief police
inspector of Ranong, Lieutenant General Sudjai Yanrat, explained the
high concentration of Burmese women in brothels there as follows:

> In my opinion, it is disgraceful to let Burmese men
> frequent Thai prostitutes. Therefore I have been flexible
> in allowing Burmese prostitutes to work here. Most of
> their clients are Burmese men.[18]

Conservative estimates of Burmese girls and women working in
brothels in Thailand now range between twenty thousand and thirty
thousand, with approximately ten thousand new recruits brought in each
year. A non-governmental organization (NGO) monitoring the trafficking
in Mae Sai estimates that an average of seven Burmese girls a day were
brought into Thailand through the Mae Sai immigration point alone in
1992.

---

[17] Hnin Hnin Pyne, *AIDS and Prostitution in Thailand: Case Study of Burmese
Prostitution in Ranong*, unpublished thesis, May 1992, p.24. See also "Ranong's
Constructive Engagement Poses Big Dilemma," *Bangkok Post*, September 13, 1992

[18] "Ranong Brothel Raids Net 148 Burmese Girls," *The Nation*, July 16, 1993.
Ranong is the only town in which Burmese women and girls in the brothels
reported the majority of their clients as Burmese. This is due primarily to the
large Burmese male migrant population working in the fishing industry.
According to an article entitled "Ranong's 'Constructive Engagement' Poses Big
Dilemma," *Bangkok Post*, September 13, 1992, one hundred thousand Burmese are
employed on trawlers and another twelve thousand work in factories in Ranong.

Economic Factors

The flourishing trade in Burmese women and girls in Thailand must be understood in the context of economic conditions in both countries. In Burma, there has been perceptible economic growth in urban areas such as Mandalay and Rangoon since the early 1990s, a direct result of SLORC's decision to loosen some government controls over trade. In the countryside, however, there has been a steady deterioration in the rural economy, with declining productivity, decreasing availability of basic commodities, such as cooking oil, skyrocketing prices, and heavy taxation. Rural villages face ever more dire poverty -- hence the attraction of work in Thailand.

The overvaluation of the Burmese currency, the kyat, also fuels the exodus to Thailand. One US dollar is worth 6.7 kyat by the official exchange rate, 100 kyat on the black market. Any foreign currency, including Thai baht, is preferable to the Burmese currency.

On the Thai side, the steady supply of illegal Burmese workers stokes a burgeoning economy nationwide with a 1992 growth rate of close to eight percent;[19] a border boom brought about by the increased trade with Burma; and a profitable tourist industry.

Burmese and Thai border towns, as noted above, have been flourishing economically since SLORC, in search of hard currency, opened its borders (and its natural resources) to Thai businesses. The growth has generated an increased demand for labor and services, in the fields of construction, food processing, fishing, commercial agriculture, and prostitution. In early 1993, the regional army commander in Ranong complained of police crackdowns on illegal immigrants. He said the crackdowns "could scare away the immigrant workers and seriously affect the local economy, which needed the cheap labor to sustain its growth."[20]

The boom, together with the tourist industry, has increased the demand for women, especially for young girls, free of infection. According to one source, tourism generates some $3 billion annually, and

---

[19] "The Straight And Narrow", *Far Eastern Economic Review*, August 5, 1993.

[20] "Leniency Pleaded for Illegal Burmese Working in Ranong," *The Nation*, February 21, 1993.

sex is one of its "most valuable subsectors,"[21] employing anywhere from 800,000 to two million people throughout the country.[22]   The Burmese women and girls are thus only a fraction of the total. Burmese trafficking and health researcher Hnin Hnin Pyne notes that in 1989,

> Tourism, which has been an increasingly profitable industry...exploded, becoming the country's major source of foreign exchange, surpassing even exports such as rice and textiles.   Thailand's image as a "sexual paradise" plays a significant role in this tourist boom.[23]

However, the tourist trade is less a factor in the sex industry than the local demand. It is estimated that seventy-five percent of Thai men have had sex with a prostitute, and that forty-eight percent experienced their first sexual intercourse with a prostitute.[24] The potential for profit and incentive to "look the other way" -- is high.

Brothels are a hugely lucrative business. Despite expenses incurred in employing a network of agents to recruit new workers, paying protection money to police[25] and giving minimal daily

---

[21] Steven Schlosstein, *Asia's New Little Dragons*, Contemporary Books, (Chicago:1991), pp.196-7. The author notes that of 4.3 million people who visited Thailand in 1988, three-quarters were unaccompanied men.

[22] Various Thai government ministries and officials estimate approximately 500,000 registered prostitutes working in Thailand. The Thai NGOs however, estimate that at least two million women and children are working in prostitution in Thailand, given that the majority of brothels and prostitutes in them are unregistered. "Prostitution: Looking Beyond the Numbers," *The Nation*, July 11, 1993.

[23] Pyne, *AIDS and Prostitution in Thailand*, p. 17.

[24] Pyne, *AIDS and Prostitution in Thailand*, p.19.

[25] A survey found that standard fees paid by brothel owners to police in southern Thailand depended on the size of the brothel: 3000 baht ($120) for ten women, 5000 baht ($200) for up to 20 and 10,000 baht ($400) for more than twenty. See "Those Greasy Palms: A Case of Criminal Greed...Or a Matter of Simple Survival," *The Nation*, January 17, 1993.

allowances to the women and girls, the brothel owners can make substantial profits. The owners collect anywhere from 100 to 250 baht ($4 to $10) per client. A typical brothel employs several dozen workers, each taking some six to ten clients a day, twenty-five days a month. The workers generally receive a little over 25 baht ($1) a day from the owner as an allowance and can keep tips from their clients, about 20 cents per man. With these meager resources, they must cover their own expenses for food, clothing, personal effects and medicine. The owner, who frequently owns more than one brothel, clearly stands to make an enormous amount of money. Agents, local police and others involved in the business also benefit.

Immigration Policy

The trafficking in women must also be viewed against the background of migration into Thailand from Burma more generally. As noted earlier, the deteriorating political and economic situation in Burma has spurred a significant outflow of Burmese into Thailand: students fleeing imprisonment in Burma, ethnic minorities fleeing counterinsurgency operations, and economic migrants, including some of the women and girls lured into brothels. Thai government officials have given estimates ranging from 200,000 to 500,000 Burmese living illegally in Thailand, and all illegal immigrants are vulnerable to abuse.

The problems of Burmese men, women and children, are particularly striking because in many cases, their entry into Thailand is facilitated or actively encouraged by Thai officials eager to attract cheap labor or make a personal profit.[26] At the same time, the fact that they are in the country illegally becomes a potent form of control in the hands of their employers, because if they protest, refuse demands or disobey, they can be summarily arrested under the Thai Immigration Act and eventually deported.

The Immigration Act is often used not to keep Burmese from entering Thailand, but to ensure compliance and obedience once they are there. This is particularly true in the case of women and girls trafficked into prostitution, who in virtually every case enter Thailand with the

---

[26] See for example the comment of the Ranong police inspector, quoted on p.79 below, who warned that a campaign against illegal immigration could ruin the local economy which depended on Burmese labor.

knowledge and complicity of border guards and police. Most are forced to remain in the brothels because of their debt to the owner and their fear of arrest as illegal immigrants.

Under the Thai Immigration Act of 1979, as amended in 1980, illegal entry into Thailand is a criminal act, punishable by detention of up to two years or fines of up to 20,000 baht ($800). Among the eleven categories of persons to be denied entry under Section 12 of the law are:

> -- those not in possession of valid travel documents, although Section 13(2) of the law exempts from carrying passports "citizens of the countries having common borders with Thailand who temporarily cross the border in compliance with the mutual agreement made between Thailand and those countries."

> -- those without means of subsistence

> -- those seeking work as unskilled laborers

> -- those who have engaged in prostitution, trading in girls or children, drug trafficking, or other immoral activities.[27]

Burmese women in the brothels can run afoul of any of the above provisions. Aiding and abetting illegal entry is a more serious crime than the entry itself, punishable by up to ten years in prison. In theory, Thai prisons should be full of the agents, recruiters and officials who benefit from or turn a blind eye to the steady stream of Burmese. They are not.

Over and above the use of the Immigration Act as a form of control, all Burmese suffer from its arbitrary and discriminatory enforcement. Members of some Burmese groups opposed to SLORC operate with the knowledge and protection of central or local Thai officials, for example, while others are more prone to arrest, detention

---

[27] Immigration Act 1979, translated by International Translations, Bangkok, Thailand, p.229.

and deportation.[28] Burmese workers in certain industries -- saw mills along the border, for example, or the tourist industry in Chiangmai -- are less vulnerable to arrest and deportation than women and girls working in brothels who become the target of highly publicized "crackdowns," in part because the industrial workers are not easily replaced and earn enough to pay the requisite bribes.

Fear of arrest as an illegal immigrant is especially pronounced among Burmese because it can mean deportation back to a country with one of the most abusive governments in Asia. For the women and girls who are victims of trafficking a particular set of problems arises. If they are arrested under the Immigration Act and sent to the Immigration Detention Center in Bangkok, they often face further sexual abuse as described in Chapter V. The IDC and other detention centers where many illegal immigrants end up are substandard, overcrowded, and characterized by corruption, extortion and physical abuse. If the women are deported, they face not only the possibility of forced conscription on the Burmese side of the border, but also arrest in Burma on charges of both leaving the country illegally and engaging in prostitution. To avoid deportation, many look for any way to stay in Thailand -- which makes them particularly vulnerable to renewed exploitation by the brothel agents.

The problem for Burmese women is also exacerbated by the fact that Thailand has no coherent policy on asylum-seekers. As far as Burmese are concerned, Thai authorities make little meaningful distinction between those who have a valid claim to refugee status and those who do not.[29] The result is that deportation decisions for the

---

[28] Amnesty International, "*Thailand - Concerns About Treatment of Burmese Refugees*", ASA 39/15/91, (London: Amnesty International, August 1991), p.4.

[29] The Thai government has been more willing to grant Vietnamese, Cambodian and Laotian refugees temporary asylum until third country resettlement can be arranged. In the case of Cambodians, the Thai government allowed more than 300,000 refugees to live in camps along the border for over a decade from 1979-92, but they were also politically useful to the government as a buffer against Vietnam-controlled Cambodia. According to Vitit Muntarbhorn, in *The Status of Refugees in Asia*, (Oxford:1992); "Those who stay in the government-directed camps are, in principle, in detention, but are generally exempted from application of immigration law and are accorded temporary

most part ignore considerations of how deportees are likely to be treated on their return to Burma. Corruption makes a mockery of those decisions in any case, since virtually anyone can avoid deportation for a price.

B. RELEVANT NATIONAL AND INTERNATIONAL LAW

Prior to the abolition of slavery in Thailand by King Rama V in 1905, prostitutes were recruited from the slave markets and sold either as "slave wives" or "slave women."[30] Slavery's abolition brought about an immediate increase in prostitution, as former women slaves were drawn into the sex trade. From 1905 until 1960, prostitution was legal in Thailand, regulated primarily by the Control and Prevention of Venereal Disease Act of 1909 (VD Control Act), which established government control over prostitution through a system of licensing and fees and required registered prostitutes to be "free of infectious disease."[31]

The VD Control Act provided that brothel owners "must get approval from the government and secure a license;"[32] that "no girls shall be forced to stay in the business against her will;"[33] that brothel operators "must not confine a prostitute;"[34] and that "the girls must be

---

refuge subject to resettlement in third countries or repatriation."

[30] Sukanya Hantrakul, "*Prostitution in Thailand*", paper presented at the Women in Asia Seminar Series, Monash University, Melbourne, July 22-24, 1983. According to Hantrakula slave wife "was completely monopolized by her husband" whereas a slave woman "would have to entertain other men if ordered by her master." She further notes that both slave wives and slave women were distinguished from prostitutes "on the basis that the latter were commonly shared by all men."

[31] Control and Prevention of Venereal Disease Act (1909), Section D (3) (c)

[32] Section A(1)

[33] Section A(4)

[34] Section A(8)(c).

at least fifteen years of age."[35]   Penalties were provided "for anyone who seduces or forces a girl to enter or remain in prostitution."[36]

According to a 1957 paper prepared by Morris G. Fox, then a U.N. Social Welfare Advisor, from 1905 through 1957 prostitution was "big business" in Thailand and the under-registration of both brothels and prostitutes was common. A recent preliminary study by the Foundation for Women, found that in the years 1957, 1958, 1959 and 1960, the number of registered prostitutes arrested were 524, 344, 308 and 298 respectively. During the same years, the number of illegal or unregistered prostitutes arrested was 6,747, 8,990, 9,400 and 7,876 respectively.[37] Then, as now, there was a "special premium for virgins." Ninety percent of the prostitutes were reported to be between the ages of fifteen and twenty, averaging about five clients a night. The vast majority were Thai, although some were "Chinese and other nationalities."[38]

The 1928 Anti-Trafficking Act

The presence of foreign nationals in the Thai brothels led the government to pass a 1928 law expressly prohibiting trafficking in women and girls. According to the Trafficking in Women and Girls Act (Anti-Trafficking Act), any person who brings women or girls into Thailand for the purpose of having sexual intercourse with other persons, and any person who is involved illegally in the trading of women or girls brought into the country for such purposes, will be liable to not more than seven years imprisonment or a fine of not more than 1,000 baht

---

[35] Section A(8)(d).

[36] Section C.

[37] Kobkun Rayanakorn, "*Study on Laws Relating to Prostitution and Traffick in Women*," a preliminary study published by the Foundation for Women (Bangkok, 1993), p. 10.

[38] Morris G. Fox, "Problem of Prostitution in Thailand," in *Social Service in Thailand*, Department of Public Welfare, Ministry of the Interior, (Bangkok: Mahaadthai Press) 1960. Originally submitted to Department of Public Welfare, February 26, 1957.

($40 in 1993 currency) or both.[39] Women and girls trafficked into Thailand are exempt from imprisonment or fine, but must be sent to a state reform house for thirty days, a period that can be extended by a judge.

The absolute prohibition on trafficking clearly distinguished it from prostitution, which was legal at the time. However, when prostitution was itself criminalized in 1960, this important distinction blurred. As a result, key protections for trafficking victims under the Anti-Trafficking law, for example exemption from fines and imprisonment, were not available under Thailand's Anti-Prostitution Law, and have been ignored. Although these protections should urgently be made available, the Anti-Trafficking Act also needs serious reform. The Foundation for Women notes that the Act does not prohibit trafficking in boys, nor does it address the selling of Thai women and girls outside of Thailand. Finally, the Act's proscribed punishments are very light and no minimum penalty is established for traffickers. Trafficking victims, meanwhile, are remanded to a penal reform institution for not less than thirty days.

1960 Criminalization of Prostitution

The clear failure of the VD Control Act meaningfully to suppress illegal prostitution, coupled with the drafting at the United Nations of the 1949 Convention for the Suppression of the Traffick in Persons and the Exploitation of the Prostitution of Others, eventually led to the criminalization of prostitution in Thailand. In 1960 Thailand adopted the Suppression of Prostitution Act (hereinafter the Anti-Prostitution law), still in effect today, which outlaws prostitution and penalizes both prostitutes and those who procure prostitutes or benefit from their exploitation. According to historian and women's rights activist Sukanya Hantrakul, the ban culminated in a social purification campaign driven by Field Marshal Sarit Thanarat, who ruled Thailand in the late 1950s and early 1960s. Sarit believed that "uncleanliness and social impropriety...led to the erosion of social orderliness...."[40] Eliminating prostitution was one

---

[39] Rayanakorn, p. 11.

[40] Sukanya Hantrakul, "Thai Women: Male Chauvinism 'a la Thai'," *The Nation*, November 16, 1992.

of his main obsessions.[41]

Under the new legislation, prostitutes were liable for imprisonment of not more than six months or a fine of not more than 2,000 baht ($80) or both; procurers for imprisonment of not more than three months or a fine of not more than 1,000 baht ($40) or both; and brothel owners for imprisonment of not more than one year or a fine of not more than 4,000 baht ($160).[42]

The law was intended, at least in theory, to criminalize prostitution. But its main purpose -- and the thrust of the majority of its provisions -- was the reform of prostitutes. Sections 11 to 16 of the 1960 Act provide that convicted prostitutes "should be given medical treatment, vocational training or both," be "committed to an assistance center [for a period] not exceeding one year from the day the person has satisfied the sentence of the court," and be penalized if they seek to flee the center by "imprisonment for not more than three months or fine of 1,000 baht or both." The Act further empowers the Director General of Public Welfare "to issue rules on disciplinary and work regulations for assisted persons," and to punish those breaking these rules by "(1) confinement...of not more than fifteen days...or (2) cutting off or reducing benefits or facilities provided by the assistance center."[43]

Since its inception this law has been denounced by many Thai women's rights advocates as weak, ill-defined and discriminatory. Penalties for procurers under the Anti-Prostitution law are lower then those under the Penal Code (discussed below). The definition of "places of prostitution" contained in the law is extremely vague and therefore largely unenforceable. The law does not explicitly exempt persons forced into prostitution from punishment and, finally, it penalizes prostitutes, but not their clients.

Moreover, as noted by Hantrakul, the Anti-Prostitution law

---

[41] Hantrakul notes that Sarit abhorred prostitution, but himself bought more than one hundred women as "minor wives." The term refers to three categories of wives delineated in the now abolished Law of Three Seals. The first category was "parental-consent wives," the second wives who wed married men to become "minor wives," and the third women in financial difficulty bought by men.

[42] Suppression of Prostitution Act 1960, Sections 6, 9 and 10.

[43] Suppression of Prostitution Act, 1960, Sections 11 to 16.

depicts prostitutes as women in need of "moral rehabilitation."[44] The law explicitly provides for the early release of the convicted prostitute who "has reformed...."[45] In Hantrakul's view, the law represents a de facto institutionalization of discrimination against women in Thai society, suppressing "female promiscuity," but tolerating similar behavior in males.

The Entertainment Places Act and the Penal Code

The government's commitment to suppressing prostitution was called into serious question a scant six years after the Anti-Prostitution law's passage with the introduction of the Entertainment Places Act of 1966. This act regulates nightclubs, dance halls, bars and places for "baths, massage or steam baths which have women to attend male customers," by requiring them to obtain operating licenses from local police. The use of such licensed establishments for prostitution is expressly outlawed, but police enforcement is lax and many "places of service" do not bother to register at all.

The Entertainment Act's passage coincided with a national policy to increase state revenue from tourism, particularly from the "Rest and Recreation"(R&R) activities of U.S. armed forces stationed in Vietnam. According to researcher Hnin Hnin Pyne, the presence of U.S. Army bases in Thailand "stimulated the growth of massage parlors, hired-wife services and bars for soldiers."[46] In 1967, one year after the passage of the Entertainment Places Act, Thailand and the U.S. military agreed to allow American soldiers stationed in Vietnam to visit Thailand for R&R. According to researcher Tranh Dam Truong, "[I]n 1967 it was estimated that the spending of the U.S. military personnel on R&R in Thailand came to approximately five million dollars. By 1970, the amount rose to approximately twenty million dollars, or as much as one-fourth of total

---

[44] Hantrakul, "Thai Women: Male Chauvinism 'a la Thai'," *The Nation*, November 16, 1992.

[45] Suppression of Prostitution Act, Section 16.

[46] Pyne, *AIDS and Prostitution in Thailand*, p.19.

rice exports for that year."[47] According to Hanktrakul

> Scrutinizing the Entertainment Places Act one could not help but
> conclude that it was enacted to pave the way for whorehouse to
> be legalized in the guise of massage parlors, bars, nightclubs, tea
> houses etc.[48]

The Anti-Prostitution and Entertainment laws developed alongside the
Thai Penal Code, adopted on November 13, 1956,[49] which did not
prohibit prostitution, but did criminalize procurement for the purpose of
prostitution and assigned higher penalties to this offense than those
contained in the Anti-Prostitution law. The Code, as amended, specifically
outlaws procurement, both forcible and not, of women for "indecent acts"
and the abduction of women for the same. Article 282 provides that

> any person who in pandering to the wanton desires of other
> persons, undertakes to furnish, seduce or persuade for the
> purpose of obscene acts, a woman, with or without her consent,
> shall be liable to one to ten years imprisonment and a fine from
> 2,000 - 20,000 baht.

Article 283 further punishes any person who

> undertakes to furnish, seduce or persuade for the purposes of
> obscene acts...by any fraudulent or deceitful means, threat,
> violence, exercising undue influence or coercion, shall be
> punished with imprisonment from five to twenty years and a fine

---

[47] Thanh Dam Truong, *Sex, Money and Morality: Prostitution and Tourism in
Southeast Asia*, Zed Books, ltd. (London, 1990), p. 161.

[48] Sukanya Hantrakul, "Archaic Prostitution Act Must Go," *The Nation*,
November 9, 1992.

[49] Vicha Mahakun, "A Brief History of Thai Law," trans. Vitit Muntarbhorn,
in *The Legal System of Thailand*, The Law Association for Asia and the Western
Pacific, 1981, p.24.

from 10,000 - 40,000 baht.[50]

Penalties increase if either offense is committed against girls under eighteen years old and again if committed against girls under fifteen years old.   If such offenses are committed against a descendant or a person under the offender's "tutorship, guardianship,or curatorship," the punishment is increased by one third.

The Penal Code also severely penalizes rape, which it defines as an extra-marital offense, and punishes sexual intercourse with minors, providing in section 277 that

> Any person who commits an act of rape on a girl aged under 15 years, who is not his wife, with or without the consent of such a girl, shall be liable to imprisonment from four to twenty years and fine from 8,000 - 40,000 baht.
>
> For wrongdoing pursuant to the proceeding paragraph against a girl aged under 13 years, the perpetrator shall be liable to imprisonment from seven to twenty years and fine from 14,000 - 40,000 baht.

The section sets forth higher penalties for gang rape or rape with a deadly weapon of under age girls. It also establishes that criminal liability can be eliminated for rape of a girl over thirteen but under fifteen, with the girl's consent, if "subsequently the Court has permitted the man and girl to get married."[51]

By 1990, Thailand had at least four separate legal regimes addressing various and sometimes overlapping components of both trafficking and prostitution. The Immigration Act also contains relevant

---

[50] Penal Code of Thailand, 1956, translated by Luang Dulya Sathya Patived, Sections 283, as amended.

[51] Ibid., section 277, as amended.

prohibitions.[52]   As a result, inconsistencies and even contradictions emerged: the Penal Law severely penalizes persons who have sex with minors, the Anti-Prostitution law does not; the Anti-Trafficking law exempts women trafficked into prostitution from imprisonment or fines; the Anti-Prostitution law makes no such exemption; the Suppression of Prostitution Act penalizes prostitution, the Entertainment Places Act, at least indirectly, regulates and even taxes it. These inconsistencies, while clearly not insurmountable, undermined the development of a clear legal sanction on prostitution and trafficking and, to some extent, contributed to several Thai governments' utter failure actually to suppress or even meaningfully control prostitution and/or trafficking, both of which rapidly expanded in the period between 1960 and 1990.

However, the root cause of the Thai government's failure rigorously to combat prostitution and trafficking as required by law lies not as much in the inconsistencies among the relevant statutes, as it does in the Thai government's routine failure to enforce even the most straightforward prohibitions, like those penalizing procurement or statutory rape or trafficking in women and girls. According to Vitit Muntarbhorn, an associate professor of law at Chulalongkorn University in Bangkok, in the period from 1960 to 1991

> ...many governments...tried to stem the tide of prostitution but much has also resulted in lip service. More often than not, they seem to wait for a catalytic incident...before pushing the authorities to take action and where action is taken the fervor dies down after a period.[53]

To a large extent this fact reflects the tension inherent in Thai policy between abhorring and prohibiting prostitution, while at the same time

---

[52] The Thai Immigration Act provides that any person who "brings or takes an alien into the Kingdom...shall be imprisoned for not more than ten years or fined not more than 100,000 baht ($40)." It also provides that any person who is aware of an alien's illegal entry into Thailand, but "despite such knowledge provides accommodations, hiding place or assistance...shall be imprisoned not more than five years and fined not more than 50,000 baht [$2,000]."

[53] Vitit Muntarbhorn, "A Scourge in Our Midst," *Bangkok Post*, November 13, 1992.

promoting and profiting from tourism which, explicit or implicitly, includes sex tourism, and from the local demand for commercial sex.

This has proved to be particularly true for Thai law enforcement officials who routinely profit from the Anti-Prostitution and Anti-Trafficking laws' non-enforcement by extorting protection fees from brothel owners or independent prostitutes. The 1992 U.S. State Department Country Reports on Human Rights Practices found that "senior [Thai] government officials have cited corruption as a major factor in police willingness to turn a blind eye to the problem. Reliable sources report that police can earn $120-200 per month in protection fees."[54]

International Law

Thailand has yet to ratify or accede to most of the international human rights instruments relevant to trafficking in women and girls, particularly the Convention for the Suppression of Traffic in Persons and of the Exploitation of the Prostitution of Others (The Trafficking Convention) and the International Covenant on Civil and Political Rights (ICCPR). On March 29, 1993 Prime Minister Chuan Leekpai publicly announced that his government

> is undertaking the necessary steps for Thailand to accede to the International Covenants contained in the International Bill of Human Rights, thus consolidating further the efforts made by previous Thai governments.[55]

As of January 1994, however, the process of accession was not complete, and the Chuan administration had made no discernible effort to ratify or accede to the Trafficking Convention.

Since 1985, however, the Thai Government has been a party to

---

[54] United States Department of State, *Country Reports on Human Rights Practices 1992* (Washington D.C: U.S. Government Printing Office,1993), p. 667.

[55] Opening Address by His Excellency Mr. Chuan Leekpai, Prime Minister of Thailand at the Asian Regional Meeting on Human Rights, 29, March 1993, Bangkok.

the Convention on the Elimination of All Forms of Discrimination Against Women (CEDAW), which obligates states parties to eliminate discrimination and, under Article 6, to take all appropriate measures to suppress all forms of traffick in women. While CEDAW does not set forth what measures states parties should institute with regard to the suppression of trafficking, earlier conventions that address trafficking of women should give content to CEDAW's directive.

The international community first denounced trafficking in the Trafficking Convention, which was approved by the General Assembly in 1949. The Convention calls on states parties to punish traffickers and to protect all persons against such abuse. The Convention also calls on states parties "so far as possible" to "make suitable provisions for [trafficking victims'] temporary care and maintenance;" to repatriate persons "only after agreement...with the State of destination," and, where persons cannot pay the cost of repatriation, to bear the cost "as far as the nearest frontier."[56]

Despite its failure to ratify many of the other pertinent international conventions, Thailand has clear obligations under customary international law with regard to many of the violations documented in this report. International law clearly condemns slavery and slave-related practices. It is well established that the prohibition of these practices has attained the status of customary international law.[57] Under customary international law the Thai authorities are also obligated to protect against and punish prolonged arbitrary detention and torture or cruel, inhuman or degrading treatment or punishment.[58] Resolutions adopted by the United Nations General Assembly also urge member nations to conform to basic principles of due process, enumerated in the ICCPR and elsewhere.

---

[56] Convention for the Suppression of the Traffic in Persons, Article 19.

[57] M. Cherif Bassiouni, "Enslavement as an International Crime" Journal of International Law and Politics, Vol.23 (New York University, 1991) p.445.

[58] Restatement (Third) of the Foreign Relations Law of the United States, Section 702 (1987).

C. The Current Crackdown: The Anand and Chuan Administrations

The Anand Panyarachun administration, installed in 1991[59] following the Thai army's overthrow of the civilian government of Chatichai Choonhavan, sought to respond to the rising prostitution and trafficking problem, particularly forced and child prostitution. In response to the escalating scare of acquired immunodefiency syndrome (AIDS), Dr. Saisuree Chutikul, then Minister to the Office of the Prime Minister for Women, Children, Youth, Education and Social Development, introduced a bill seeking to legalize prostitution by women eighteen years or older, who work voluntarily and regularly check their health. In attempting to legalize voluntary prostitution, Dr. Saisuree sought to strengthen law enforcement in the area of compulsory and, particularly, child prostitution and trafficking. However, the bill lapsed following the end of Anand's administration after the March 1992 elections and, as with previous administrations, the endeavor to address prostitution faltered. Nonetheless the Anand administration did put in place some notable reforms with ramifications for forced and child prostitution and trafficking.

Most notably, Anand established a unit within the Crime Suppression Division (CSD), a division of the Central Investigation Bureau that has national jurisdiction. The CSD is empowered to make criminal investigations and inquiries anywhere in the country.[60] The CSD's newly formed anti-prostitution task force was charged with rescuing those forced into slavery, in particular children compelled into prostitution.

Unfortunately, the CSD's task force was plagued from its inception with problems of understaffing and inadequate funding. According to the former task force head, Police Colonel Bancha

---

[59] Prime Minister Anand served from just after the February 1991 coup until April 7, 1992 when he was replaced by General Suchinda Kraprayoon. Demonstrations in May 1992 forced Suchinda to step down. Anand returned as prime minister until new elections were held in September 1992 when Chuan Leekpai took over leadership of a coalition government. The second administration of Anand is commonly referred to as Anand II.

[60] "The Administration of Justice in Thailand", Thai Bar Association, 1969, pp. 47-48.

Charusareet, his unit was

> supposed to raid every brothel that has child prostitutes or
> detains unwilling girls for prostitution anywhere in the country,
> but it has a staff of only six people and one vehicle.[61]

The Division's efforts were further hampered by the lack of cooperation
from the local police officers in whose jurisdiction the CSD was mandated
to intervene. Other local analysts also accused the CSD units with
inconsistencies in their work and taking bribes from brothel owners and
other police units.

Nonetheless, in 1991 the *Bangkok Post* reported nine brothel raids
by the police.[62] According to researcher Pyne, out of these (and other)
raids a new trend began to emerge: "[o]ver 200 of the 342 women
discovered came from Burma."[63]   Pyne notes that the Center for
Protection of Children's Rights (CPCR), which maintains a shelter for
women and children rescued from the brothels, estimated that in 1991,
ten to twenty percent of the prostitutes were Burmese. The increase in
the number of non-Thai women and girls, particularly among those
brothels most associated with involuntary and child prostitution, signaled
a rise in trafficking of women into the country for the purposes of
prostitution.

The presence of Burmese women and girls in Thailand's most
abusive brothels was increasingly evident in 1992. Statistics for 1992
compiled by CPCR estimate that roughly thirty to forty percent of the
children they assisted were Burmese.[64]   Major CSD/police raids on
several brothels in Ranong in June and July 1992 turned up an estimated
153 Burmese women and girls.[65] Raids earlier in the year had rescued

---

[61] Police Colonel Bancha Charusareet, *The Nation*, November 11, 1992.

[62] Pyne, *AIDS and Prostitution in Thailand*, p.2.

[63] Ibid.

[64] Center for the Protection of Children's Rights, (1992 Statistical Review of
Persons Assisted by the Center) unpublished.

[65] "Burmese Girls Tormented in Thai Brothels" *Bangkok Post*, July 31, 1992.

an additional 147 women and girls.[66]

The increasing presence of foreign nationals in these raids prompted the Anand administration to take another notable step to address this problem. Initially, according to researcher Hnin Hnin Pyne, most of the Burmese caught in the government raids in 1991 were either deported immediately or transferred to the Immigration Detention Center in Bangkok to be deported three to six months later.[67] However, reports of deported women and girls being arrested upon return to Burma for prostitution or illegal immigration, and unconfirmed statements that some HIV positive returnees were murdered by Burmese authorities, raised concerns about summary deportation for both NGOs and the Thai government.

Faced with this dilemma, Dr. Saisuree Chutikul tried to develop an alternative to the Burmese women and girls' summary deportation. Rather than arresting and imprisoning the girls as illegal immigrants, Dr. Saisuree arranged for at least one group of them to be sent to the penal reform institution of Pakkret[68] pending an officially sanctioned repatriation in cooperation with the Burmese authorities. From June through July 1992, the majority of the Burmese women and girls "rescued" from brothels were sent to Pakkret.[69]

---

[66] "Cyanide Jab Reports Halt Deporting of Burmese Girls," *The Nation*, April 2, 1992.

[67] Pyne, *AIDS and Prostitution in Thailand*, p.25.

[68] Ban Pakkret is located on an island in the Chao Phraya River in Nonthaburi, just outside Bangkok. It was established in 1960, pursuant to the Anti-Prostitution Act, as a reformatory for Thai prostitutes. There are four such reformatories in Thailand run by the Ministry of Interior's Public Welfare Department. Two are located in Bangkok: Ban Pakkret and Ban Kredtakarn. The other two are in Nakorn Rathchasima and Lampang. "Pakkret" has become the generic name to describe the entire penal reform system. These institutions can accommodate about 2,500 women each year.

[69] Thus, from the June 1992 raid involving twenty-nine Burmese, six of the girls (young or pregnant) were housed with a local shelter, while the remaining twenty-three were sent to Pakkret. In the July 7, 1992 raid, involving seventy-nine Burmese women and girls, thirteen young or pregnant girls were sent to an NGO shelter in Bangkok, and the remaining sixty-six were sent to Pakkret. By

The Thai NGOs working with trafficking victims supported Dr. Saisuree's attempt to find an alternative to the arrest and summary deportation of the Burmese women and girls as illegal immigrants. However, they argued that the Dr. Saisuree's plan was problematic both because the penal reform institutions are discriminatory in nature and unduly punitive, and because the safety of the women and girls upon return to Burma could not be monitored or guaranteed.

Dr. Saisuree, who after the September 1992 became an adviser to the new Chuan government, defended the Pakkret scheme. In an interview she gave to an NGO called End Child Prostitution in Asian Tourism (ECPAT), she argued that the Burmese women and girls posed a problem for Thai authorities because they were in the country illegally and possessed no papers. They were not classified as refugees because they did not flee their country of origin. Under existing Thai law they had no legal right to remain in Thailand. She disputed NGO contentions that the women and girls faced dangers on their return to Burma, citing assurances from SLORC that the women and girls would not be harmed and could be visited subsequent to their return to establish their well-being.[70] Although she pledged that all 150 women and girls in Pakkret as of mid-1992 would be repatriated at Thai government expense[71] in late September, only ninety-five of the 150 Burmese women and girls were officially repatriated.

It was in this context that on November 2, 1992, Prime Minister Chuan Leekpai announced to provincial governors that he intended to crack down on child and involuntary prostitution, and child labor abuse. He told the governors of Thailand's seventy-five provinces that they must "take responsibility and give special attention to child prostitution and

---

late summer 1992, more than 150 Burmese women and girls were housed in Pakkret. Most of the women and girls we interviewed were among this group.

[70] "Saisuree Defends Plan To Repatriate Burmese Women," *The Nation*, August 20, 1992.

[71] "Ambassador Seeks Return Home Of Burmese Women," *Bangkok Post*, July 31, 1992.

child labor abuse."[72] Several days later, the Minister of Interior, General Chavalit Yongchaiyudh, announced that he wanted all brothels shut down in two months.[73] In subsequent speeches, the Chuan administration pledged to get "concrete results" in three months.[74]

In large measure, Chuan's announcement came in response to growing national and international condemnation of child and forced prostitution, particularly in the wake of the 1992 raids. It was also prompted by efforts, particularly by the United States Congress, to deny trade preferences to countries making use of child or forced labor.[75] The Thai government highlighted these latter concerns in announcing the crackdown and the Prime Minister told local journalists that "Thailand's trading partners would boycott our products if these two problems continue to exist."[76]

In making his announcement Chuan was careful to distinguish between forced and child prostitution and prostitution more generally. He clearly stated that he would not attempt to touch prostitution in general, telling reporters

> I won't talk about what is impossible, if the problem cannot be solved, I won't order the authorities to tackle it.[77]

---

[72] "Chuan Demands End To Child Exploitation," *Bangkok Post*, November 3, 1992.

[73] "Chavalit Wants All Brothels Closed," *Bangkok Post*, November 7, 1992.

[74] "PM Gives Himself 3-Month Deadline To Curb Child Sex," *The Nation*, November 14, 1992.

[75] Pursuant to the FY 1994 U.S. Appropriations Act for the Department of Labor, the U.S. Secretary of Labor is directed to undertake a review to identify foreign industries that utilize child labor in the manufacture or mining of products exported to the U.S.

[76] "Trade Worries Driving Prostitution Background," *The Nation*, November 15, 1992.

[77] Prime Minister Chuan Leekpai quoted in "PM Gives Himself 3-Month Deadline To Curb Child Sex," *The Nation*, November 14, 1992.

Instead, Chuan argued that the numbers of child and forced prostitutes were smaller and the problem therefore easier to address.

Chuan's announcement was greeted by local activists with a measure of optimism, particularly because he pledged, for the first time in the history of Thai government crackdowns on forced or child prostitution, to address the involvement of government officials in such abuse. He told the governors that in some areas of Thailand the problems were caused by police and military officers and noted that Thailand's "problems...will be less if the ones who have the weapons and enforce the law are not the sources of the involvement."[78]

Not all Thai police welcomed Chuan's plan. Soon after Chuan's announcement, Deputy Police Director General Police General Pongammart Amartayakul told reporters that sex-related crimes would probably increase if the brothels were shut down. He reportedly said that men in the seaside provinces would have "a lot of pent-up sexual aggression" and would have to relieve themselves. He suggested that the rate of rapes and other sex-related crimes might rise as men find no place to satisfy their "sexual desires."[79]

The Chuan administration must be commended for undertaking such a high-profile effort to combat involuntary and forced prostitution, which by definition includes trafficking, and for publicly acknowledging the involvement of government officials in perpetrating and profiting from such abuse. However, in the year since Chuan's November 1992 announcement, several serious problems have emerged with his policy that raise questions about the depth of the government's commitment to end forced and child prostitution. Where the Burmese trafficking victims in particular are concerned, that policy may have exacerbated the problem.

First and foremost, the trafficking of Burmese women and girls into Thailand continues, virtually unchecked. Moreover, despite clear evidence that Thai law enforcement and immigration officials remain directly involved in the flesh trade, not a single officer has been prosecuted or punished for such abuse. Brothel owners, pimps and

---

[78] "Chuan Demands End To Child Exploitation," *Bangkok Post*, November 3, 1992.

[79] "Police Chief Links Brothel Ban with Rise in Sex Crime," *Bangkok Post*, November 11, 1992.

recruiters have also been largely exempt from punishment. In fact, the main targets of the Chuan administration's crackdown on forced and child prostitution have been the victims themselves.

Some of these problems might have been avoided had Chuan undertaken the necessary legal reforms and adopted the relevant international instruments. Local women's rights NGOs have proposed a number of reforms in the existing Anti-Trafficking and Anti-Prostitution laws that would, among other measures, stiffen the penalties for trafficking and procurement for prostitution, reduce or remove the remand of prostitutes or trafficking victims to penal reform institutions, and clearly punish clients who engage in statutory rape. Unfortunately these legal reforms have yet to become law. In addition, while Thai NGOs have called on the Chuan administration to ratify or accede to ICCPR and the Trafficking Convention, both of which would provide clear guidelines for addressing trafficking and compulsory prostitution, neither ratification has been actively pursued by the government.

Even in the absence of such legal reform, however, Thailand's existing national and international obligations could yield more effective and equitable results. As noted above, the existing Anti-Prostitution, Trafficking and Penal laws clearly penalize recruitment and a range of other abuses associated with trafficking and forced and child prostitution, and Thailand's obligations under CEDAW provide clear guidance with regard to eliminating both discrimination and trafficking. Thailand's existing laws also clearly protect the victims of forced and child prostitution, and of trafficking in particular, from imprisonment, fines and summary deportation. Unfortunately, the Chuan administration has failed to issue a clear mandate to its law enforcement officials to enforce these prohibitions. As a result, police are routinely tolerating traffickers and arresting trafficking victims on charges of prostitution and illegal immigration, although as a matter of both fact and law they should not be liable for either crime.

The crackdown's problems might have been mitigated had the Thai government created procedural mechanisms to ensure that corrupt police were penalized and forced and child prostitutes and trafficking victims were treated fairly. Instead, and over the objections of local NGOs, the Chuan administration weakened one of the key official mechanisms, the Crime Suppression Division, which although not without problems of its own, had the authority to override local police and to deal with forced and child prostitution directly. Instead Chuan, in late 1992, disbanded the CSD's anti-prostitution task force in favor of a new CSD "Coordination Center for the Prevention and Suppression of Child Prostitutes and Child Labor Abuse," which was mandated to maintain a database on brothels. The Coordination Center was required to carry out the raids and rescues in cooperation with other local police units, many of which local NGO observers suspect "are actively involved in the sex trade or on the payroll of the brothel owners."[80] In addition, the Chuan administration appears to have abandoned the non-punitive, coordinated, official repatriation of Burmese women and girls entirely.

Thus, in the months following Chuan's November 2, 1992 announcement, the myth that his administration is "rescuing" forced and child prostitutes has been shattered. Except for the few women and girls whom NGOs are able to take to emergency shelters, it is clear that government's high profile "rescues" actually are arrests.

---

[80] *The Nation*, December 26, 1992.

III. THREE PORTRAITS

The following portraits of three women give some idea of the experiences of women and girls caught in the trafficking. These women were interviewed in NGO shelters over several hours and the descriptions given here come directly from their testimony.

"LIN LIN"

When "Lin Lin" was thirteen years old, her mother died and her father remarried. Shortly thereafter, her father took her from their village of Chom Dtong near Keng Tung to Mae Sai. She was too young to get an identity card in Burma, so her father paid 35 kyats ($.30) for a travel pass. They arrived at a job placement agency in Mae Sai and her father was given 12,000 baht ($480) from the agent who assured him he could find a job for "Lin Lin" in Thailand. [That payment became the basis of Lin Lin's bondage to the owner.]

"Lin Lin" was sent with Thai Lu, a Shan woman living in Thailand, on a bus to Bangkok. The agent from Mae Sai met her at a hotel in Bangkok and took her and Thai Lu to Kanchanaburi.[81] She was brought to the Ran Dee Prom brothel and on the third day told to work.

"Lin Lin" did not know what was going on until the man started touching her breasts and body. He took her to a room and told her to take off her clothes, then forced her to have sex. "Lin Lin" thought perhaps her father knew what kind of work was in store for her, but she herself was completely unaware.

"Lin Lin" was kept in Kanchanaburi to work for one month and then sent to Korat[82] to a brothel owned by the sister of the Ran Dee Prom brothel owner. She stayed at the Juja Hotel 109 for nine months. Afterwards, she was sent to another brothel in Kanchanaburi for three months, owned by another relative.

There were over one hundred girls in Kanchanaburi of whom

---

[81] Kanchanaburi is west of Bangkok towards the Burmese border.

[82] Korat is northeast of Bangkok.

over half were from Burma and about twenty were less than sixteen years old. In Korat, there were about sixty girls with some ten from Burma and twenty who were less than sixteen years old. In Korat, "Lin Lin" was the youngest, but there were even younger girls in the brothels in Kanchanaburi.

The arrangement was the same in each brothel. The owner provided room and food, but everything else was added to "Lin Lin's" debt. She was allowed only to keep her tips. She heard from the other girls that she got about forty percent of the amount each client paid deducted from her debt, but she never saw the accounts or was ever told the amount or details of her "debt."

In all three brothels, "Lin Lin" sat in a windowed room with a number and the clients paid the owner 100 baht ($4) per hour for the number they wanted. Clients could take her out all night for 800 baht ($30) by leaving an identity card or passport at the brothel. During the weekdays she had six or seven clients a day, but on the weekends the number rose to fourteen or fifteen a day.

She saw police in all the brothels in which she worked. They seemed to know the owners very well and were often around with their uniforms, guns and walkie talkies. They also took the girls often to the rooms or out for the whole night.

After thirteen months in Kanchanaburi and Korat, "Lin Lin" agreed to a 5,000 baht ($200) loan to return to Mae Sai for a visit. The loan was for the bus ticket and escort; she never received any cash. When she arrived in Mae Sai she did not have enough money to get all the way home. A couple came up to her and asked her name and said they would help her get home. She agreed and waited for them. When the couple arrived there were four other girls in the car. "Lin Lin" got in and was driven back into Thailand. On the road to Chiangrai, the driver paid a policeman in uniform at a checkpoint. In Chiangrai, the girls were delivered to another agent who had two more girls. All seven of them were then driven to Klong Yai.[83]

In Klong Yai "Lin Lin" worked with forty other girls and women. About fifteen others were from Burma and almost all of them were sixteen or seventeen years old. The owner told "Lin Lin" she owed him for her transportation from Mae Sai to Klong Yai and her living

---

[83] Klong Yai in Trat Province is along the Thai-Cambodian border just across from the Khmer Rouge trading town of Pailin.

expenses. She assumed she also needed to get at least 5,000 baht ($200) so she could pay for the transportation home. She also assumed all the owners knew each other and had investments in each other's brothels. She had no idea what she owed to whom.

In Klong Yai "Lin Lin" worked in a restaurant and the men picked out which girl they wanted. "Lin Lin" saw the owner and pimps slap the girls often; she herself was slapped in the face and often warned that she had better do whatever the client wanted. She had to work every day and was only allowed two days off a month when she had her period.

She did not go to the doctor because she had to pay the expenses herself and it cost 200 baht ($8). Once when she had pus and pain in her vagina, she went to the doctor, but she had to borrow money from the owner for the medicine. This amount was added to her debt.

In Klong Yai the police had special arrangements with the owner and could take the girls for free. There were many policemen at the restaurant every night, some in full uniform and others without, but all with guns. They took "Lin Lin" many times without paying. Once when Lin Lin was out with another girl and two policemen for the whole night, the other girl insisted that her client use a condom. The policeman in question put a gun to her head and refused.

"Lin Lin" was never allowed to refuse a client. If she tried, the owner and pimps would tell her, "If you don't pay back your debt, you can stay here forever." She was warned she would be beaten if she ever came out of the room before her client. She never tried to run away; she was afraid the owner would follow her or her family because she had not finished paying off her debt.

"Lin Lin" said that in Klong Yai the brothel was ordered closed by government authorities in November 1992, and the pimps stood outside the door. The clients would still come and negotiate what they wanted with the pimp, leaving an identity card or passport for collateral. The girls stayed in other houses and were collected or delivered to their clients. The clients could take her anywhere they wanted, and "Lin Lin" was often sent out alone, sometimes deep into the jungle.

On January 18, 1993, the Crime Suppression Division (CSD) raided the brothel, as journalists watched and took pictures. The CSD arrested about twenty-seven girls, but no owners or pimps. The brothel was closed at the time, and the police came to the houses where the women and girls were staying and arrested them. They were not allowed to get any of their belongings and "Lin Lin" only had the clothes she was wearing. She was first brought to the Klong Yai police station and transferred the same day to a police station in Bangkok. The next day she was released to the NGO shelter with eleven others under the age of sixteen.

"Lin Lin" said she did not understand much about AIDS. Some clients used condoms, but sometimes the condoms broke; other clients refused to use them. She said she was tested several times for AIDS but was never told the results.

"NYI NYI"

"Nyi Nyi" is from a small farm outside of Keng Tung. She came to Thailand when she was seventeen years old with a friend who had worked in Bangkok before and invited her to go back with her. "Nyi Nyi" never knew what kind of work she would get and never imagined it would be prostitution.

When "Nyi Nyi" arrived in Mae Sai with her friend and sister, the agent gave her 15,000 baht ($600) in advance which "Nyi Nyi" gave to her sister. An hour later, "Nyi Nyi" and the friend left in a truck driven by a policeman to Chiangrai. The policeman was in uniform, carried a walkie talkie, and "Nyi Nyi" assumed he had a gun. There were many police checkpoints between Mae Sai and Chiangrai. "Nyi Nyi" said she was very scared, but her friend assured her that the policeman had everything arranged, and they would not have any problems. The policeman took them to a hotel and told them to wait until the agent came to collect them.

The next day, the agent from Mae Sai arrived and brought them to the Dong Saen Tea Shop. ("Nyi Nyi" never knew where in Bangkok the tea shop was located.) Shortly thereafter, her friend escaped, leaving "Nyi Nyi" alone and frightened. She said she thought about how her brother used to tease her that she was so quiet and easily fooled that one day, someone would sell her. He was right, she thought.

At the brothel she was told she had to repay the 15,000 baht ($600) debt. "Nyi Nyi" never understood that the money the agent gave her was a debt. She assumed it was simply a gift to her family while she was away. The owner bought many things for her in the beginning and told her they were all "free," but later she learned every purchase had been added to her debt. Everything she ate and used in the brothel was added to her bill. She never knew how much she owed or the terms for repaying it. She knew that there was a chance that at the end of the two years, she might have nothing to show for her work.

"Nyi Nyi" and the other girls had to work from 11:00 A.M. to 3:00 A.M. unless they had clients, then they had to work until they were finished. She took days off only when she had her period. Very occasionally, she said, she refused men who were very drunk and dirty, but the brothel owner had a good heart and never beat her.

Every morning around 9:00 A.M. the owner's wife asked each girl how much money she wanted for the day. "Nyi Nyi" always took as little as possible, 20 to 30 baht ($0.80 to $1.20). She used her tip money for expenses and gave all her extra money to the owner to keep safe, so that she could eventually take it home. She thought she had 2,000 to 3,000 baht ($80 to $120) saved with the owner.

She could go out of the brothel to buy food, but she never ventured very far, nor did she ever dare to talk to anyone. She was always afraid the police would arrest her. She could not speak Thai, could not read or write and did not know where she was in Bangkok or how to get back home. If she had money, she thought, she could probably hire someone to take her away from the brothel, but she had none. There was no telephone at the brothel, and "Nyi Nyi" would not have known how to use one if there was.

The policemen were always in and around the brothel and knew the owner well. They often chose girls to take to the rooms but never "Nyi Nyi" -- fortunately, she said, because she was afraid of them.

One day, after "Nyi Nyi" worked for about one year, her agent told her she had paid her debt, but with only about 400 baht ($16) extra in savings, she had not earned enough to cover transportation costs back to Burma, let alone money to live on when she got there. The owner had promised her that she could go home for Songkran (the Thai and Burmese new year) in April 1993, but she was arrested first.

On July 12, 1992 at 9:00 P.M., four plainclothes policemen from the Crime Suppression Division came to the brothel. They took one girl upstairs, then came down and closed all the doors. "Nyi Nyi" lost everything she had, as none of the girls or women arrested were allowed to get their belongings. Between fifty and sixty girls and women were arrested, together with one pimp. "Nyi Nyi" did not know what happened to the couple who owned the brothel. At the police station, the arrested girls and women were told that the owner had called and offered to bail them out but that they would be taken back to Burma instead.

The police asked each of those arrested for her name, age and address and told them all that they could go home in two or three days. Later the same night, "Nyi Nyi" and the others were transferred to Pakkret, a reformatory for prostitutes set up under the Anti-Prostitution Act of 1960. "Nyi Nyi" spoke of Pakkret as a jail where the Burmese wore purple uniforms and the Thai blue. For most of the six months she was there, "Nyi Nyi" was sick with a high fever. She had no way to communicate with anyone outside, since she was illiterate. In any case, since only visitors with identification cards and permission could visit detainees at Pakkret, none of "Nyi Nyi's" friends would have come, since they were also illegal immigrants.

"Nyi Nyi" was tested once in the brothel and again in Pakkret for AIDS, but she was never told the results. She said she would like to know if she was HIV positive so she could use condoms to prevent spreading the disease, although she has never seen any condoms in Burma and does not know if they are available. She learned about AIDS in Pakkret and is afraid she has it. She was frequently sick and when we interviewed her, she had lost over thirty-three pounds in six months. She never had an injection or met a doctor before she came to Thailand and never knew what to do when she was sick. The only health care she received was medicine taken from the shelf in the brothel on the advice of other girls and women there.

"Nyi Nyi" told us she wanted to go home but did not want anyone to take her all the way back because they would see how her family lives. "Even though I worked like this, " she said, "I still couldn't do anything for my family. I am so embarrassed and ashamed."

"SWE SWE"

"Swe Swe" is from a farm in Wan Bao village near the Chinese border. She came to Thailand when she was seventeen years old with two other friends to find work as maids or laundresses. She did not tell her parents she was going to leave the village because she knew they would not agree.

"Swe Swe" sold her ring for 2,070 kyats ($20) and 40 Chinese yuan (five dollars). She later converted this to 300 baht ($12). Her friend had five silver coins. They took a car to Mae Sai and had to pay all baht they had plus three silver coins.

Once in Mae Sai, a Burmese man asked them where they were

going and warned them they could be arrested by police. He said he could help them find work. "Swe Swe" and her friends were not sure they trusted him but knew the risk of arrest was real. They agreed to refuse his offer and try to find Saen Sai Lu, a place known back in their village for its employment possibilities. By the end of the day, after they had been unable to find it, the same Burmese man reappeared, and they agreed to put themselves in his hands. They were then put in a van with two other girls and taken Bangkok via Phayao. They passed through many police checkpoints but were never stopped.

When "Swe Swe" arrived in Bangkok, a brothel agent gave her 9,000 baht ($360) to buy clothes and other personal effects. She still had no idea she was being tricked, because she and her two friends were taken to be maids at the agent's house. At the end of the week, all three were brought to the brothel.

"Swe Swe" did not even realize it was a brothel until she was brought to a room, still with her sarong on.[84] She said she screamed and kept hitting her head against the wall as her first client forced himself on her. Afterwards, her head was bleeding badly; she said she remembered little else.

"Swe Swe" was too afraid to escape when she realized that she was working in a brothel. The owner and agents were always warning her not to go out because she would get stolen or arrested. She had no idea where she was or how to get home. She could not speak or read Thai. The owner and agents kept telling her to stop crying because the police would hear her. She felt helpless. Her parents had told her that something like this could happen if she left the village, but she did not believe them. The other girls tried to comfort her by saying that they had worked in the brothel for a few years already and that everything would be all right.

---

[84] A sarong is a traditional Asian long skirt.

IV. TRAFFICKING IN WOMEN AND GIRLS

A. RECRUITMENT

The first phase of the illicit trade in Burmese women and girls is their recruitment and sale into brothels throughout Thailand where they are compelled to prostitute themselves under conditions tantamount to slavery. The actions of the recruiting agent and the brothel owners are clearly in violation not only of international standards on trafficking and forced labor, but also of domestic Thai laws prohibiting trafficking and prostitution. Yet for the most part, these laws are not enforced.

In her pathbreaking study of Burmese women in Thai brothels, Hnin Hnin Pyne classified her subjects by their means of entry into prostitution: voluntary, bonded and involuntary.

> Voluntary indicates that the woman, prostitute-to-be, approaches the owner/manager of a sex establishment herself; bonded implies the involvement of parents or guardians, who receive money from an agent or owner for giving away their daughter; and involuntary conveys the use of deception and coercion of the women by an agent or owner/manager.[85]

All but one of the women we interviewed for this report were lured from their homes on a promise of economic benefits. But data from other sources, including police records, indicate that in Ranong in particular, the use of physical force to procure women and girls is common.

We interviewed thirty Burmese women and girls in depth, twenty-six of whom had been trafficked into Thailand through Mae Sai, one who had come through Mae Sot, and three who had been brought in through Ranong. Of the thirty, nineteen had parents or guardians who were peasant farmers or farm laborers.[86] They came from villages all

---

[85] Pyne, *AIDS and Prostitution in Thailand*, p.23.

[86] Of the remainder, two were orphans brought up respectively by a laundress and an assistant midwife; one's father was a lumberjack; one came from a family of small shopowners; and four came from families where the occupation of the parents was not clear.

over Shan State (Taichelek, Keng Tung and Taunggyi); Kachin State
near the Chinese border; Kayin State; Sagaing division in central Burma;
and even Rangoon, the capital city. They ranged in age from twelve to
twenty-two, with the average age around seventeen; only four had ever
been to school and could read or write in their own language.

The process of recruitment by agents working for brothel owners
is necessarily covert, because of laws restricting the freedom of Burmese
citizens to leave their country and laws in both Thailand and Burma
making prostitution a crime. The brothel owners thus rely on a network
of "small agents" and "big agents", acting in concert -- and for a price --
with Thai and Burmese officials to keep a steady supply of Burmese girls
coming across the border.

The Promises

The lure for the Burmese girls is the chance to escape from
poverty. Twenty-nine of the thirty women and girls interviewed
deliberately set out to earn money in Thailand for themselves or their
families. Only four of these knew when they set out from home that they
would be involved in some form of prostitution. Of the twenty-five others,
eighteen thought they would be working as maids, cooks, laundresses,
waitresses or some other job that required few skills. Like seventeen-year-
old "Tin Tin" who was invited by a friend to go to Chiangrai to make
flowers, or sixteen-year-old "Tar Tar" who was brought to Thailand by a
teacher on the promise of making enough money to buy a traditional
dress, most were attracted by the promise of an opportunity to help their
parents or simply to escape from the grimness of their own surroundings.

A Burmese girl, aged fourteen or fifteen, from the Akha ethnic
group told a Thai NGO worker how the agents operate:

> ● One day two women came to the village while "Par"
> was on her way to the fields. They talked to her about
> how much better it would be to live in the city and work.
> [They talked to her father as well.] Her father wanted to
> go along, as he was afraid of her being sold, but the two
> women said it was not necessary and would be a waste of
> his time. So her father did not go and her mother cried,
> because "Par" was her only daughter. Ah Daw [the agent]
> told her that the daughter would be fine. She would be

taking care of children and would get to go to school. Ah
Daw's husband came and said the same thing. Finally,
"Par's" parents believed Ah Daw. Ah Daw told her that
she would study Thai for a month, then learn to speak
Thai, make necklaces, take care of children. Ah Daw gave
her father 800 baht ($32).[87]

In only two cases we investigated did the girls return voluntarily
to prostitution after they had been returned home. In one case, the girl
believed that since she had lost her virginity anyway, she might as well
earn money for her family. In the other case, the shame of being known
in her village as having worked as a prostitute was too great, and she,
too, decided to help her family by going back.

In only one case out of the thirty we investigated directly was a
girl lured from her home on other than a promise of economic
prosperity.

● One family, in Wan Mai, south of Taunggyi in Shan
State, had two daughters. "Htet Htet" was sixteen years
old and unmarried; the younger one, age thirteen, had
been married to a man in drug warlord Khun Sa's
territory, in the town of Bing Nong. A man from Bing
Nong had come to the family's house to tell them that
their daughter there was sick. The family agreed to send
"Htet Htet" to visit. "Htet Htet" went with the man, but
instead of taking her to see her sick sister, he took her to
Thailand.

Of the thirty girls and women, eleven had been brought into
Thailand by family members. The network for finding work in Thailand
appears to be well-known in the rural areas of Burma that supply the
women and girls. Relatives knew, for example, to take their daughters or
sisters to the "Mekong shop" in Mae Sai or to a particularly well-known
agent or to a certain temple. In some cases, women who have returned
from Thailand provided the information to potential recruits. In other

---

[87] From detailed interviews with twenty-one Burmese girls and women
conducted by an NGO in Chiangmai which requested anonymity. Human Rights
Watch spoke at length with the person who had conducted the interviews.

cases, relatives who live in or near Mae Sai knew the agents and directed the new recruits to them.

Of the remaining nineteen women and girls, eight were recruited by women returning from the brothels, who saw their escape as contingent on their ability to find successors. Those women were likely to reinforce the belief at home that they had worked as waitresses or maids in Thailand to save face. They would emphasize the cash rewards rather than the abuse. Four of our interviewees were recruited by someone known to them in the village, such as a teacher, who was operating as a "small agent" for the "big agent" in Mae Sai. Two set out for the border themselves, without knowing anyone at the other end. It is unclear how the remaining women were recruited.

The Money

For all but two of the twenty-six Burmese women and girls trafficked through Mae Sai, the cash transaction that sealed the recruit's fate took place in the town of Mae Sai itself, the point of entry into Thailand. (In the other two cases, the "small agent" made direct payments to the girl's family in her village.) In most cases, the girls, accompanied by parent, brother, aunt, friend or teacher, met the agent on the Thai side of the border, where the agent gave the girl's companion a sum ranging from 1,000 to 20,000 baht ($40 to $800). The average seemed to be about 5,000 baht ($200). It is not clear whether this payment was understood by the recipient as a recruitment fee, a gift, a purchase (of the woman or girl), reimbursement for travel expenses or a cash advance to buy clothes and other necessities. The terms of the payment were never explained to the woman or girl. It only became clear once she was in the brothel that the owner perceived it as credit against future earnings that she must work off, with interest. In at least one case, it seemed as though the Mae Sai agent functioned as a regular moneylender; while the daughter was working in a brothel in Klong Yai, the agent who had originally given 5,000 baht ($200) to the father reportedly loaned the father another 20,000 baht ($800) at his request. The daughter was to be kept in thrall to the brothel owner until the additional loan was paid off.

Once the money changed hands, the Mae Sai agent often arranged through the local police to send the woman or girl, usually with two or three other new recruits, sometimes with as many as ten, in a truck or van directly to a brothel or to another agent at a way station en route to Bangkok -- usually Chiangrai. Of those we interviewed, twenty ended up in Bangkok. Two went to brothels in Samut Sakhorn; one to Klong Yai near the Thai-Cambodian border; one to Prachinburi; one to Kanchanaburi; one to Chiangrai; one to Mae Lim (Chiangmai province) and three to Ranong.

Sexual Abuse in the Course of Recruitment

Even before they reach the brothels, the women and girls are subject to sexual abuse, including rape. In general, rapes during recruitment may be discouraged by the fact that virginity increases the value of the girls and women to a brothel owner -- and thus, presumably, to the recruiting agent who supplies him or her.[88] Of the thirty girls and women we interviewed, three reported being raped en route to the brothel; one in Chiangrai, one in Burma en route to Ranong and one on the road to Songkhla.

> ● When "Chit Chit", for example, left her village in Taichelek in 1990 at the age of eighteen, she was taken directly to a policeman named Bu Muad in Mae Sai who himself was the brothel agent. He gave her 10,000 baht ($400) and drove with "Chit Chit" and another woman from the same village to Chiangrai in a police van. Another agent drove the truck. The two women stayed for eleven days with the policeman and his wife, who lived in Chiangrai, before going on to Mae Lim, in Chiangmai, where the brothel was. While they were in Chiangrai, the policeman raped "Chit Chit" while his wife and the other woman were at the market. He warned her that if she ever told anyone, he would beat her. She was afraid of him because he always carried his gun. According to "Chit Chit", this policeman was a regular visitor to the brothel in Chiangmai, beating girls for the owner if they did not cooperate or were recalcitrant in any way.

---

[88] It is true, however, that "virginity" is as much a marketing ploy by brothel owners as it is a physical state: women and girls are frequently advertised as "virgins" for many nights, even weeks, after the initial penetration.

● "Kyi Kyi", a twenty-year-old woman from Rangoon, was invited by Ye Htun, a man she had known in the market where she worked with her mother, to work at a restaurant in Tavoy (in the Tenasserim Division of southern Burma, midway between the city of Moulmein in the north and Ranong in the south). She agreed to go, as long as she could bring a friend with her. The two women and Ye Htun stopped en route to Tavoy at Moulmein where they stayed in a guesthouse for two days. On the second night, according to "Kyi Kyi", Ye Htun raped her. He then took the two on a small boat, not to Tavoy but to Ranong, where Ye Htun sold "Kyi Kyi" to the Victoria brothel for 6,000 baht ($240).

● Another woman, "Nan Li Li" whom we met in the Immigration Detention Center (IDC) in Bangkok, but who had been so traumatized that she was unable to speak, had been befriended by another woman, "Muyar" at the IDC. "Muyar" told us "Nan Li Li" was Shan, twenty-three years old and originally from Keng Tung. She had been taken by an agent from Mae Sai to Chiangrai and flown from there to Hat Yai, a trading town on the Thai-Malaysian border, with a woman escort and two other girls. From there she was sent with a driver to Songkhla, only to be raped by the driver en route. After three days in Songkhla, she was arrested and taken back to Hat Yai where she tried to escape. She was captured and detained first in Songkhla and then in the IDC, and was widely believed to be "crazy."

Girls and women are also subjected to various forms of sexual abuse short of rape.

● When "Tar Tar's" teacher first brought her to the agent in Mae Sai she was taken into a separate room. The agent said he had to check her virginity -- "Tar Tar" said he did so by touching her breasts and crotch to see "how sensitive she was."

Moving From Brothel to Brothel

The initial destinations of trafficking victims are rarely final; while some women and girls do stay in one brothel for a year or more, many of those we interviewed were frequently moved around by the owners.

- "Tar Tar", for example, spent twenty days at the Rong Ram See Tong brothel on Soi Payana in Bangkok; she was then transferred to the Rong Ram 46 on Tawit Soi 1 where she worked for three or four months. She then moved to Rong Ram 48 for two months and Rong Ram 84 for three months. All four brothels appeared to be run by either a single owner or a network of owners who among them employed five hundred girls, most of them Thai.

- In another case, "Yin Yin", aged twenty-one, decided to seek work in Thailand in 1992. Accompanied by two other girls and her mother, she traveled from a village in Muang Piak to the district town of Taichelek (Burma). From there, they went by car to an agent in Mae Sai. "Yin Yin" had worked with a relative frying fish in Mae Sai six years earlier, for a period of about six months, so the family already had contacts in the town. The agent advanced 25,000 baht ($1,000) to "Yin Yin" who gave all but 1,500 baht ($60) to her mother. She stayed with the agent for two days, then was taken by a policeman, together with the two girls from her village, to Chiangrai. They stayed overnight at a temple. The next morning, "Yin Yin", her two friends, the agent from Mae Sai, a driver, and the owner of a brothel in Bangkok called the Pai Mai Tea Shop, drove by van to the tea shop. "Yin Yin" worked in Bangkok for ten days. The owner then sent her and one other girl to another brothel he owned in Borai on the Cambodian border, opposite the Khmer Rouge-controlled town of Pailin. She was in Borai for six months before being taken back to Bangkok -- by the original agent from Mae Sai -- to the

Dao Kanong brothel where she stayed for six or seven months. "Yin Yin" believed the owner had at least ten brothels, with about eighteen agents operating out of Dao Kanong alone where about fifty women and girls worked.

Ranong

Of the three women we interviewed who entered Thailand from Kawthaung and were delivered to brothels in Ranong, none received any money in advance. All three claimed they were effectively sold to the brothel owner by "friends" who turned out to be agents for a price ranging from 2,000 to 7,000 baht ($80 to $280). The three said they received no money at all from either the agent or owner.

None of the women we interviewed had been forcibly kidnapped, but we obtained enough information from other sources to suggest that the practice is not uncommon. In June 1991, for example, police from the Crime Suppression Division raided a brothel in Ranong's Muang District and "rescued" twenty-five women, most of them Burmese. Two of the women were sisters who, intending to go shopping, had hired a motorcycle to take them to the Ranong market. The motorcycle driver abducted the two and sold them to a brothel. According to a police report filed by the girls' uncle, they were forced to work and threatened with death by the pimps if they tried to escape.

In another case we investigated, a fifteen-year-old girl from Shan State was interviewed by a Thai NGO in October 1992. She had been working in Thai brothels since she was ten. She said that she had been looking after a water buffalo near her home when a man grabbed her and put her in a car, then took her to Keng Tung. She ended up in a brothel in Chiangmai for the next five years; the man who abducted her received 35,000 baht ($1,400). Because she was kidnapped, the owner apparently thought she would try to leave, so she was kept locked up whenever she was not working.[89]

---

[89] See footnote 87.

B. THE BROTHEL

As noted above, entertainment places, such as massage parlors, bars and night clubs are considered legal if registered with the government. The girls and women working there have some ability to negotiate the terms of their employment and the nature of the interaction with their clients. Brothels, which can range from seven or eight girls in the back of a noodle shop to a multi-story building with over a hundred workers, are, by contrast, illegal.

In the brothels, the owners use a combination of threats, force, debt bondage and physical confinement to control the women and girls, force them to work in deplorable, abusive conditions, and eliminate any possibility of negotiation or escape. Those seeking to flee legitimately fear capture and punishment by the owners or agents, arrest for illegal immigration or prostitution or abduction and resale to another brothel owner. The clients of the Burmese we interviewed were predominantly Thai, but included foreign workers from neighboring countries such as Burma, Cambodia and Malaysia. According to our interviews, only when the girls were sold as virgins for high prices were clients from wealthier countries involved.

Many of the Burmese women and girls are sold to agents of the brothels by friends or relatives who themselves may be unaware of the nature or conditions of their employment. As noted above, the payment they get from the agent becomes the core of a debt which the women must pay off through prostitution before they are allowed to return home. The debt, often compounded with one hundred percent interest, is the cornerstone of the control exercised by the brothel owners and pimps over the women and girls. None of the women and girls we interviewed understood the nature or extent of their debt. It had never been explained to them. In most cases, they had no idea how much they owed nor could they explain to us the terms of repayment.

Debt Bondage

Debt bondage is one of a number of slavery-related practices set forth and defined in the Supplementary Convention on the Abolition of Slavery, the Slave Trade and Institutions and Practices Similar to Slavery of 1949. The Convention defines debt bondage as the status or condition arising from a promise made by an indebted person to provide personal services or the services of a third party where the length and nature of the services are not limited or defined or the reasonable value of the services are not applied to the debt.[90] Under customary international law, states must eradicate and make criminal the practice of debt bondage, even if they are not party to the Supplementary Convention, its predecessor or related conventions.

Debt bondage is also prohibited by international law on forced labor[91] and by Section 344 of the Thai Penal Code which states that

> Whoever dishonestly induces, by means of deception, ten persons upwards to perform any kind of work for him or for a third person with intent not to pay wages or renumeration to such person, or with intent to pay such persons lower wages or renumeration than those agreed upon shall be punished with imprisonment not exceeding three years or fine not exceeding six thousand baht, or both.

Yet despite these clear prohibitions every Burmese woman and girl we interviewed reported this abuse.

For most of the women interviewed, that debt appeared to consist of the amount they received from an agent of the brothel owner at the Thai-Burmese border, plus transport, protection money or payoffs to police and other officials and any advances given for clothing or other personal items.

The money given to the girl or woman, her family or a secondary agent at the border (in Mae Sai, a standard payment was 10,000 baht [$400]) was typically doubled by the brothel owner to include "interest". None of the Burmese girls or women we interviewed knew of the arrangements between the brothel owner and the agents, but they assumed the "interest" was at least in part the agent's profit. Many of those interviewed had no idea how much money was exchanged and as a consequence had no idea how much they were indebted. All of the

---

[90] Supplementary Convention on the Abolition of Slavery, Section I, Article 1 (1957).

[91] Universal Declaration, Articles 4 and 5 and International Covenant on Civil and Political Rights, Article 8.

Burmese were continually reminded that not only did they have to pay off their debt, but also whatever living expenses they were unable to meet from their meager tips.

Some women never knew how much they earned, how much they were supposed to earn, or what the terms for repayment of the debt were. Even those who did have some idea of the debt/payment arrangement, were not any better off for the knowledge. For example,

> ● "Tar Tar" knew that the going rate in one of the places she worked, the Dao Kanong brothel in Bangkok, was 110 baht ($4.40) per hour. She was told by other women in the brothel that her share was thirty percent, or 36 baht ($1.40) plus any tips from the clients. "Tar Tar" figured of the 36 baht, half went toward repayment of her original cash advance, which was 10,000 baht ($400, doubled to include interest), and half was ostensibly for rent and food, so "Tar Tar" was never actually able to keep any of it. The owner gave her and the other workers 30 baht ($1.20) a day to buy food, but this amount also was deducted from her earnings. She did keep track of how much she had earned, but assumed that she and the owner would settle accounts at the end of the year.

> ● Another woman, "Sein Sein," who was sent to Bangkok when she was sixteen years old, had a similar arrangement. The standard fee for clients was 120 baht ($4.80) a "time." "Sein Sein" was supposed to get a third, but she never received any money. Instead she got one chip per client and counted her chips every night to calculate the amount to be subtracted from her original debt of 10,000 baht ($400). She received 30 baht ($1.20) a day from the owner, plus tips, to pay for food and other expenses. The tips were small except for the first time when she got 300 baht ($12) from the man who took her virginity. At the time she was arrested, she had worked five months, serving ten to fifteen clients a day, and was sure she had paid off her initial debt, but there were no accounts to prove it. She had managed to save

500 baht ($20) from tips, but lost it at the time of the arrest when the police refused to let her take her belongings with her.

Some of the women had a vague understanding that they would have to work for a specific length of time to pay off the debt. "Thanda" was seventeen years old when her mother received 20,000 baht ($800) from a brothel agent in Mae Sai on the understanding that she would work for a year, although the terms of her employment were never spelled out. (She thought she was supposed to receive a third of the income from her clients, but when she was arrested after two months, all of her share was still going to pay off the debt.) The owner of the brothel warned "Chit Chit" that she had to stay one year or else he would follow her back to her village, get her back and beat her. She was so frightened she never even asked him to settle the accounts.

- In another case, "Tin Tin" was held responsible for paying back the 5,000 baht ($200) that the owner of the Sanae brothel in Klong Yai had given an agent to bring her there from the border. She had no idea when she left for Thailand that she had effectively been sold into prostitution until she arrived at the brothel, where she was given a number and told to go sit in a windowed room. When she tried to refuse, the owner, Ba Ouan, told her that with interest, she now owed 10,000 baht ($400) and said, "If you want to go home, then you've got to work, or you'll never pay back your debt."

Not only were the girls or women never told the terms of their debt, but also every worker was different: no consistent share or percentage was established for all workers within a brothel. Only two of the thirty women and girls we interviewed had been able to settle their accounts with the owner, despite the fact that some had worked in brothels for years. All were simply waiting to be told their debts were paid and hoping they would have some extra money saved from tips to pay for their transportation costs to return home.

- "Than Than" was one of the very few we interviewed who paid off her debt, but her story indicates the exploitation and arbitrariness of the process. An agent in Mae Sai had given her stepfather 10,000 baht ($400) when he agreed to find work for "Than Than." She was seventeen at the time and understood that she would be working in a restaurant. Instead, she found herself in a brothel in Bangkok. She got a red plastic chip from each client and was told that her debt would be paid off with 1,000 chips. She also understood that one- third of the clients' fee would go toward debt repayment, and that she would have to work about seven months to clear the debt. After eight months, she was told her debt was paid. "Than Than" explained that it was hard to know exactly how the debts worked as each girl had a different arrangement with the owner.

The calculations here are instructive. If "Than Than" had 1,000 clients over eight months, that means she had about 125 a month or about five men a night, assuming a twenty-five-day working month. The going rate at her brothel was 120 baht ($4.80) an hour. The gross income to the brothel owner from her work alone was thus 15,000 baht ($600) a month. If "Than Than" had been getting one third of the income and her debt remained steady, she should have been able to repay her debt after two months. If, as was the case for many of the girls, the debt was doubled to include "interest", she still should have been able to repay it in four months. Using 1,000 chips as the terms of repayment meant either that Than Than's debt was not doubled but quadrupled by the owner, or that her share of the income was -- at best -- about eight percent.

The Burmese women and girls we interviewed were determined to pay off their debt as quickly as possible, knowing that it was the only way to get home. In addition to the enforced compliance with the brothel owner's demands, therefore, there was also a financial incentive to take as many clients as possible, do what they demanded, work every day possible, accept long hours and avoid any additional expenses that might be added to their debt, especially health care with its unpredictable costs. The following cases are typical.

● "Yin Yin" was told by the brothel owner that she could go home after 1,000 clients. Most of her clients were

police, soldiers, border patrol and other men in uniform
as the brothel was located in Borai (along the Thai-
Cambodian border). "Yin Yin" worked hard and served
1,000 clients in three months. She saved about 3,000
baht ($140) in tips. Then the owner told her that her
mother had taken another 5,000 baht ($200) from the
agent. As a result, "Yin Yin" believed she was in debt
again, even though she had no way of knowing whether
her mother really did take more money, and no idea
what to do if the owner was lying. The owner then
transferred her to another brothel, this time in Bangkok,
where she had to work for another six to seven months
before she was arrested.

● When "Thazin" was eighteen years old she knew she
had to pay back the 5,000 baht ($200) she had received
from the agent and given her father at the border, but
she did not know how long it would take to do so. She
had never discussed her accounts with the owner, she
said, because she was too afraid and did not dare to ask
questions. "Thazin" knew vaguely that the job she had
taken at the border was prostitution, but she never
imagined it would be as bad as it was. All she could think
of was to pay back the money and get home. It never
occurred to her to escape because she had no idea where
she was, even after three months in the brothel. She also
did not speak Thai, and she had no money.

In two cases, Burmese girls we interviewed said they were able to send
some money back to their families, over and above their original
advances, but in neither case was it clear whether this money constituted
"earnings" or an addition to their debt. The girls clearly believed it was
the latter. In one of those cases,

● "Nwe Nwe", aged fourteen, did not take any cash
advance from the agent in Mae Sai, afraid that if she did
so, she might find herself unable to leave a job she did
not like (it was not clear whether she knew the job would
be prostitution). She was taken to a brothel in Samut

Sakhon where there were about ten girls aged fourteen to twenty and was given to understand that she would receive fifty percent of the profits. After just over a year, she was able to send 5,000 baht ($200) back to her parents through the owner, although it is unclear how or whether she knew that the money had actually reached them.

● "Nu Nu," who came to Thailand when she was thirteen years old, worked at the same brothel in Samut Sakhorn as "Nwe Nwe." She had about five clients a night who paid 200 baht a time.

If "Nwe Nwe" had a similar number of clients as "Nu Nu," the gross income per year per girl would have been 150,000 baht ($12,000). If the girls really received half of the gross, they would have been doing well by Thai standards, but they received nothing of the kind.

Illegal Confinement

The debt bondage of the Burmese women and girls is enforced by their near total confinement to the brothel premises. Such confinement violates Article 9 of the International Covenant on Civil and Political Rights which provides that no one shall be arbitrarily deprived of liberty, a norm that has achieved the standing customary international law. It also violates Section 310 of the Thai Penal Code which states that

Whoever detains or confines any person, or by any other means, deprives such person of liberty of person shall be punished with imprisonment not exceeding three years or fine not exceeding six thousand baht, or both.

If the commission of the offence according to the first paragraph causes death or grievous bodily harm to the person detained, confined or deprived of the liberty of person, the offender shall be punished as provided in Section 290, Section 297 or Section 198.

The Burmese women and girls we interviewed were kept in the

brothels on terms that clearly constitute illegal confinement. They were generally not allowed to leave the brothel or its immediate surroundings without escorts. They were threatened with a range of consequences should they attempt to do so. The brothel owner often reminded the girls and women of the extent of his network and the support of the police who could trace the women if they left before their debt was paid. Given that they generally had no knowledge of the amount they owed or the terms for repayment, they rarely ventured very far outside.

With few exceptions, the Burmese were unable to communicate with anyone outside of the brothel and its clients. In many cases, telephone and mail communication was banned by the brothel owner.

● "Kyi Kyi", who worked in the Old Victoria brothel in Ranong for three years, said she was beaten by the pimps whenever she tried to listen to the BBC or send letters out through clients.

● "Chit Chit's" mother called the brothel in Mae Lim (Chiangmai province) once, but "Chit Chit" was not allowed to speak with her. She did, however, manage to sneak letters to her relatives in Mae Sai through the post office.

● Another woman, "Yin Yin", received a telephone call from her mother. She was allowed to speak, but with the owner standing by listening.

● A fourth woman, "Sein Sein", received a call from her brother.

None of the other interviewees had any communication with their families, and many would not have known how to use the telephone if they had been allowed to do so nor knew anyone with a telephone whom they could call. The inability to send mail also meant that even when the women were able to save some money, they were unable to send it back to their families in Burma. For many of the women and girls this had been their major motivation for going to Thailand in the first place.

The primary concern of every Burmese woman and girl was to avoid getting arrested, imprisoned and deported as an illegal immigrant.

Most did not dare leave the brothel or the immediate surroundings for fear of being arrested or sold to another brothel that might not know how to get them back home. Some tried to avoid speaking so no one would know they were not Thai. Those interviewed claimed their fears were constantly reinforced by the brothel owner, agents and pimps. They were told of the terrible conditions of the Thai immigration jails, abuse during deportations and frequent arrests by Burmese officials upon return to Burma. Many of those interviewed said the news reports in April 1992 of SLORC's use of cyanide injections to execute HIV positive Burmese women returning from Thailand were used by brothel owners and pimps to scare them into staying at the brothel. (The reports have never been confirmed.) The Burmese girls and women believed that only the owner and his network, which included police, could get them home safely.

The pimps use different arguments to keep the women confined.

● "Pyone Pyone" was seventeen years old when she came to Thailand. She was told she could not leave the brothel because she was too new.

● "Tin Tin" was told, "If you go out, the police will arrest you and you have no papers. Then you will have to go to prison and never get home." As a result, she only went out of the brothel when clients bought her out for the night or she had to buy food or other necessities at nearby shops.

● "Phyu Phyu" was brought to Thailand by her uncle when she was seventeen years old. She was afraid of the police, and the owner always told her if she left, someone else would catch her, sell her again, and she would never be able to get home.

● "Thuza" was sixteen years old when she was brought to a brothel in Thailand. She tried to leave once, but the agent found her and brought her back.

Unlike the brothels in Bangkok, where the owners play on the women's and girls' fear to keep them in thrall, the brothels in Ranong use armed force and other instruments of physical control. Three brothels raided in July 1993 were surrounded by electrified barbed wire. Guards of a brothel in the city of Ranong raided in 1991 carried guns. In June 1992, after another raid in Ranong, police said that the three Thais and thirty-three Burmese women working there "had been confined to their rooms in the compound of the brothel which was fenced in with barbed wire and live electrical wires."[92]

The combination of debt bondage and illegal confinement renders the employment of the Burmese women and girls tantamount to forced labor, defined by the ILO as "All work or service which is exacted from any person under the menace of any penalty and for which the said person has not offered himself voluntarily." The Thai constitution also states "Forced labor shall not be imposed" except in response to a "public calamity" or when the country is at war or in a state of emergency.[93] Despite these prohibitions, the women and girls are clearly being forced to work as prostitutes "under menace of penalty" and are subjected not only to repeated and grievous sexual abuse but also to deplorable working condition.

Rape and Other Forms of Sexual and Physical Abuse

In large measure, the brothel owners are profiting off the repeated rape and sexual assault of the Burmese women and girls, sometimes over long periods of time. The Thai Penal Code contains articles which, had they been enforced, would have permitted the prosecution of brothel owners, agents, pimps and clients for this crime.[94] These laws routinely go unenforced.

As noted above, Section 276 of the Thai Penal Code penalizes any person "having sexual intercourse with any women...by threatening by any means...." Section 277 penalizes the rape of girls under fifteen years

---

[92] "CSD Police Free 36 Girls From Sex-Pit in Ranong," *Bangkok Post,* June 11, 1992.

[93] Constitution of the Kingdom of Thailand, Section 31, December 22, 1978.

[94] Act Amending Promulgating the Penal Code (No. 8),B.E. 2530 (1987). [As published in Government Gazette Vol. 104 part 173, September 1, 1987.]

of age, with or with or without their consent, and, with stiffer penalties, the rape of girls thirteen or younger. Section 278 outlaws "obscene acts" committed against anyone over fifteen "in the circumstances that resistance is impossible." These provisions have been rarely, if ever, applied in the context of assaults that take place within brothels, even though virtually all women and girls working there are in a circumstance where "resistance is impossible."

Many of the Burmese we interviewed talked at great length about losing their virginity by rape in the brothels. The brothels typically consist of a "selection" room or *hong du*; a room for virgins or children (*hong bud boree sut*, literally, the "room to unveil virgins"); and a series of cubicles where the clients can take the girls. The "selection" room consists of a window behind which girls with numbers sit on a bench. A client picks a number, pays between 100 to 250 baht ($4 to $10) to the owner and takes his choice to a room for the paid amount of time. The girl selected has no right to refuse her client nor does she have any control over how many clients she must take. Girls and women who had been in the brothel for years still spoke in detail about their first days in the brothel, how they tried to resist, the force used against them, how much it hurt, and how they could not stop crying. The following cases are typical:

● "Tar Tar" was sold as a virgin to a Japanese man for 12,000 baht ($480). He took her to a hotel on Petchaburi Road in Bangkok and raped her while the man's wife waited in a car outside. It was very painful, and "Tar Tar" said she screamed until she was unconscious. She thought because the room was so big and expensive, no one could hear her. She was in pain and felt a terrible burning, but the next day, she was sent to a fifty-year-old man. She tried to refuse, but the brothel owner said she had better get used to it.

● "Myo Myo" had been in the brothel for five days when she had to take her first client, a Thai, who paid 1,500 baht ($60) for her virginity. She tried to escape, but the client slapped her and held her back. She finally ran out of the room. Two pimps and the owner came and caught her. All three beat her. Another Burmese there told her to be quiet and try to do as she was told so she did not get killed. After that the owner beat "Myo Myo " often, and she said she had to agree to everything.

● When "Tin Tin" was first brought by an agent to the Sanae brothel in Klong Yai, along the Cambodian border, she tried to refuse to work as a prostitute. The owner constantly reminded her of the amount she owed him. She said she saw others who tried to refuse slapped in the face, and hit hard. After that, she never dared to say no to a client or leave the room before he did. She saw other girls come out before a client, and the pimps beat them. During the first month, she was sold to four different clients as a virgin. She said she never agreed to have sex, that it was all forced.

● "Nu Nu" was sold as a virgin in a brothel in Samut Sakorn for 5,000 to 6,000 baht ($200 to $240). After the first week, she had to take as many clients as the other girls, but instead of being given a number and sitting in the windowed room, she was kept with other young children on a bench in the back room.

● When "Myint Myint" was seventeen years old she was brought to Mae Sai by her brother and a friend who said she could get work washing dishes. She was brought to a brothel in Bangkok, and for the first month, did in fact work washing dishes at the owner's house adjoining the brothel. Every day, the owner kept telling her that she was not making any money, and she would never be able to pay back her debt until she started working at the "hotel." After a month, she did not have enough to eat and no way to pay back the debt, so she finally went to the hotel. The owner sold her virginity for 30 baht ($1.20).

The accounts of other Burmese girls interviewed by Thai NGOs are similar.

- A fifteen-year-old girl taken to a brothel in Songkhla said she was given a drug and raped while she was unconscious. She only remembers waking up with no clothes on.

- A ten-year-old girl from Shan State, mentioned above, whose kidnapper received 35,000 baht, said she was given to a *farang* (Westerner) who paid 5000 baht ($200) for her virginity. It hurt so much she passed out, and the brothel owner later beat her with a stick.[95]

For girls fifteen years old or younger, the sexual intercourse they experience in the brothels always constitutes rape, and clients should be held accountable for it. Brothel owners also are liable under the Penal Code for having assisted or facilitated the commission of this offense and should be punishable for two thirds of the penalty for statutory rape.[96]

However, rape and sexual assault are not restricted to under age girls or to the women and girls' initial experiences in the brothels. The combination of debt bondage, illegal confinement and the threat or use of physical abuse force the women and girls into sexual slavery. Many of those we interviewed made clear that they were forced to have sex for the duration of their time in the brothel. Refusal to service clients often resulted in a beating, warnings about defaulting on their debt or threats of arrest as illegal immigrants.   Long after she was first raped, for example,

- "Tar Tar" tried to refuse clients who wanted oral or anal sex, but the owner just kept warning her that she would never get home until she worked off her debt. Eventually, she realized that the more she cooperated, the sooner it would be over. She explained that the debt meant that none of the girls or women could refuse a client. Once one of her friends tried to refuse a client and the next day everyone got beaten. Some of the girls were hit in the face and had swollen mouths.

---

[95] See footnote 87.

[96] Penal Code, Section 86.

● "Tin Tin" told us that she never dared to say no to a client or leave the room before him for fear the brothel pimps would beat her up.

In July 14, 1993, when 148 Burmese girls and women were "rescued" from three brothels in Ranong, (Victoria, Wida and Sontaya), one twenty-seven-year-old woman who was six months pregnant said she was still being forced to have sex with clients. A woman named Mu Mu, aged twenty-four, who was three months pregnant, was beaten by pimps in the Wida brothel to bring on a miscarriage after she refused to have sex with a client. She was reportedly hit on the back with a club and punched in the stomach until she began to bleed. She was taken to a hospital on a motorcycle by her colleagues, and was in critical condition at the end of July.[97] The incident was confirmed by the attending doctor who told of treating a woman for a miscarriage brought on by severe beatings.[98] Many of the other women found in the brothel had bruises on their thighs and buttocks from being beaten with canes for refusing clients or trying to escape.[99]

Similar accounts came from women in Ranong after raids in 1992. Nilni, a Burmese women aged twenty, told police that she was forced to have sex within three days of leaving a local clinic where she had given birth to a baby girl.[100]

The repeated threat or use of force by brothel owners to compel the women and girls to have sex with the clients not only renders them in some instances accomplices to statuary rape, but in every single case constitutes a clear violation of the penal law prohibiting procurement for the purposes of prostitution. This law not only penalizes the initial act of procurement, both forcible and not, by which the women and girls are first recruited into prostitution, but punishes such procurement "to service the wanton desires of another...irrespective of whether or not a number

---

[97] "Ranong Brothel Raids Net 148 Burmese Girls," *The Nation*, July 16, 1993.

[98] "Ranong HIV Rate High Says Doctor," *The Nation*, July 27 1993.

[99] "From One Hell Hole to Another," *The Nation*, July 25, 1993.

[100] "42 Rescued From Brothel", *The Nation*, June 11, 1992 and "CSD Police Free 36 Girls from Sex-Pit in Ranong," *Bangkok Post*, June 11, 1992.

of such acts have been committed at different occasions." [101]

Working Conditions

Nearly every Burmese girl and woman interviewed had to be available to work between ten to fourteen hours a day with a only few days off each month during their menstruation. Some explained that they could get time off if they were very sick or sore, but they only dared request such days if absolutely necessary. Those interviewed had an average of ten clients a day (some with as many as twenty on weekends) with no means to negotiate who their clients were or what they did with them. Compliance was often obtained by threats and beatings from the brothel owner and pimps.

The girls and women could also be hired out for the entire day or night. Regular clients would leave a deposit and/or identification and take the girl or woman wherever the chose, with whomever and for as long they were willing to pay. Those interviewed talked of feeling vulnerable and frightened in these situations. Some girls reported that friends they knew in the brothels were in fact stolen through such arrangements and never heard of again. However, because of the owner's fear that his girls could be stolen and sold elsewhere, he were usually careful about which clients he allowed to take the women and girls out of the brothel.

As noted above, most women lived and slept in the same cubicles where they took their clients. The Ranong brothels raided in July 1993 were particularly bad:

> Each of the cubicles, measuring two by two-and-a-half meters contained a cement bunk where the girls were forced to prostitute themselves. Hidden doors, concealed by secret passageways where the girls could be hidden in case of a raid.... The stench of the place was terrible. There were no proper toilets. It was a hell hole. [102]

If the brothel owner gave an allowance each girl interviewed

---

[101] Penal Code, Section 282-283.

[102] "From One Hell Hole to Another," *The Nation*, July 25, 1993.

typically received 30 baht ($1.20) a day. This forced them to rely heavily on tips from their clients to supplement their income. They had to pay for all their expenses including food and health care. The amount given by the owner was hardly enough for food, especially as they had no opportunities to go to the market or cook and had to purchase ready made from nearby shops. There were also personal expenses of soap, shampoo and other toiletries. Those interviewed often reported putting off visits to doctors because they were not sure how much they would have to pay, and not purchasing medicine unless it was absolutely necessary. If they were unable to pay, they feared the amount of the bill would be added to their debt.

> ● "Yin Yin" worked from noon to midnight and served ten to twenty men a day. She had to do whatever the clients wanted and never refused them. The owner only gave her and the other workers 30 baht ($1.20) each day for food and all other expenses. This was not enough for survival. She worked every day except when she was menstruating. Sometimes when she was very sore, she asked to stop for a few days, but she tried to work as much as possible so she could pay off her debt and go home. She told us, "The owner knows he doesn't have to physically force us."

> ● One girl from Keng Tung, seventeen years old, was taken to a brothel in Hat Yai in the south, and described to an NGO worker in Chiangmai how dirty, sweaty and smelly her clients were. She did not want to sleep with any of them, but the owner beat her if she refused. She said she asked them to take a bath first, but they would not agree.[103]

Health Care, Birth Control and AIDS

Provision of health care in the brothels is sporadic at best, and in most cases non-existent. In six out of nineteen different brothels where women we interviewed had worked, they reported routine contact with

---

[103] See Footnote 87. Interview took place on September 14, 1991.

health care providers, but this was primarily to provide birth control and test for sexually transmitted diseases (STDs), including AIDS. Most brothels have minor medications and creams available for their employees, often for a price. Serious illnesses usually go untreated. When we interviewed "Myo Myo" at the Old Victoria brothel in Ranong, she was very thin and yellow and had a high fever. In the three years she had been there, she had never been to a clinic or seen a doctor.

All of the girls and women we interviewed who had been trafficked from Burma were provided contraceptives by the brothel owners; it was clearly in the owners' interest to ensure their workers did not get pregnant. The women and girls we interviewed were mostly given pills; three of those who had worked at the Dao Kanong brothel in Bangkok had depo-prevera injections from a doctor or health worker who came to the brothel. One girl in Ranong was given injections by the owner's wife. The women and girls themselves appeared to have no choice of which contraceptives they would be given nor did they understand how they worked. In at least one case, the owner found it in his interest to keep the girls from menstruating so that there would be no excuse to stop work during the month. He did this apparently by giving them improper instructions for taking the pills and never allowing them to take the one week placebo pill for menstruation.

In a group of twenty-one Burmese women at one shelter in Chiangmai, interviewed by a local NGO between 1991 and 1992, eight women were given pills by the brothel owner, four were given injections, one had to buy pills herself and one received nothing. (Information on the other seven was unclear.) One of the women given pills took three or four a day; she was never told how to use them. A girl of twelve who was given pills started hemorraghing shortly thereafter, but the brothel owner would not take her to a doctor.

None of the thirty women and girls we interviewed had become pregnant themselves. Among those trafficked in through Mae Sai, only one girl mentioned a colleague having gotten pregnant, a Shan woman who, once her pregnancy was discovered, was kept in the brothel owner's house. He arranged a marriage for her so she could deliver the baby in a hospital without questions being asked. (Abortions are illegal in Thailand, but are widely available in back rooms and local clinics.) Among the group of twenty-one women interviewed by a local NGO at the shelter in Chiangmai, one girl, aged fifteen, became pregnant two months after her arrival. She wanted an abortion, but the brothel owner would not permit it. He said if she had a boy, he would keep it, and if it was a girl, he would give the baby away.

Ranong is a different story. In July 1993, a highly publicized raid led to the "rescue" of 148 Burmese women and girls. Twenty (thirteen percent) were found to be pregnant. In one brothel in Ranong studied by Hnin Hnin Pyne, six out of twenty-four women were pregnant. Two of them had abortions at the local hospital, and for one of the two, it was her third abortion.[104] In the Let Ywe Sin brothel, according to a woman who worked there, pregnant women had to give birth in the brothel with the assistance of a midwife. Within a week of giving birth, they had to be back at work, either as a receptionist, a cleaner or a kind of housemistress for the other women. Their babies were usually sold by the brothel owner.[105]

It is not clear whether the pregnancy rate is higher in Ranong than in other provinces in Thailand because of the generally harsher conditions there. Some of the NGO staff working closely with these women explained to us that girls and women in Ranong believed that if they had a child they would be released. Thus, they tried to get pregnant. Women who were seven or eight months pregnant could be freed for 8,000 to 10,000 baht ($320 to $400), according to a woman from the Let Ywe Sin brothel.[106]

The Burmese women and girls we interviewed were more likely to contract HIV than to become pregnant, however. Nineteen of the thirty girls we interviewed had been tested for HIV in Pakkret reformatory. Of these, fourteen were found to be HIV positive. Since most, if not all, had come to Thailand as virgins, they were most likely infected by their clients. The use of unsterilized needles when they were given birth control injections, treated for infections or tested for AIDS in the brothels may also have been a factor. After the July 1993 raid on a brothel in Ranong, mentioned above, the *Bangkok Post* of July 16 reported:

---

[104] Pyne, *AIDS and Prostitution in Thailand*, p.29.

[105] Interview with women from Ranong brothels conducted by the Burmese Student's Committee for Action, August 16, 1992.

[106] Ibid.

Police expect a large number of the women from this brothel to test positive for HIV as they found that the girls had shared the same old syringes during rudimentary examinations carried out on the premises.

Public health officials have distributed condoms to brothels throughout Thailand, often free of charge. The girls and women interviewed reported that condoms were often given to the client and its price included in the rate. None of those interviewed reported any insistence by the brothel owners on condom use; it depended entirely on the client. The girls and women themselves did not know about AIDS or the benefits of condom use while in the brothel. Those interviewed also told us that using condoms was often too painful, especially when they had to service a minimum of seven or eight men a night.

The Thai Penal Code provides that whosoever, by negligence, "causes bodily or mental harm to another person shall be punished with imprisonment not exceeding one month or 1,000 baht or both."[107] The Thai government has an obligation to hold brothel owners accountable for negligence in relation to the appalling health care conditions in the brothels. The brothel owners are preventing the women and girls from negotiating the terms of sexual intercourse, denying them appropriate health care, failing to inform them about the risk of exposure to HIV/AIDS and failing to insist that the clients use condoms. As a result, they are exposing the Burmese women and girls to greatly increased risk of contracting HIV/AIDS. Clearly, the brothel owners are in a position to prevent the "mental and bodily harm" that resulting from practices, and they should be held criminally negligent for failing to do so.

Impossibility of Escape

For most women, there are rarely more than three ways to leave a brothel: escape, arrest and deportation, or return to one's village, often as a recruiter. The first is rarely a real option. The fear of being arrested as an illegal immigrant is so pervasive and control by the owner so absolute, that our interviewees thought they had no choice but to wait until the owner told them their debt was paid and rely on him or his agents to escort them back through the checkpoints and border crossings.

---

[107] Penal Code, Section 390.

Most were severely limited in their ability to speak and read Thai and feared this would mark them immediately for arrest as illegal immigrants. Moreover, with no means to contact their families, no money and no sense of where they were, they had little chance of being able to get home on their own. They clearly could not seek the help of the police, since the police were so deeply involved in the brothel operations.

Of our interviewees, only three had ever tried to escape.

● "Myo Myo" said that one time when she was caught trying to go out of the Old Victoria brothel in Ranong, the owner locked her in her room and beat her. He then sent her to the showroom and beat her again along with two other pimps in front of all the other girls. She was then sent back to her room and locked in for three days. During this time no one came in and she did not receive any food. When the door was open she was immediately sent to work again.

● "Kyi Kyi" tried to escape in 1991, but the owner caught her and took her to the kitchen and beat her with a very thin wooden stick. The owner told her if she tried to escape again he would shoot her with a gun. He then took pistol out and put it to her head saying "like this." "Kyi Kyi" has never been out of the brothel since she was brought there over two years ago.

● "Chit Chit" tried to escape after she realized how large her debt was. She left the brothel after she had received a 500 baht ($20) tip from a client. However, soon after she left, she realized she had no idea how to get home and could easily be arrested for being in Thailand illegally. She finally returned to the brothel and told us, "The owner doesn't have to lock us up because he knows we can't go far since we don't have any identification cards and never enough money."

Among a group of twenty-one women interviewed by an NGO in Chiangmai, one girl, aged fifteen, tried in 1991 to escape from a brothel in Songkhla where she was frequently beaten for refusing customers. She got a ride with a driver who said he was going to Bangkok, but he dropped her off in an unfamiliar place. It appears to have been in Songkhla or close by. She was confused and went to a noodle shop. The owner called the police who came to get her. After four or five days there, the police told her she would either have to stay at the police station indefinitely or go back to the brothel. She decided to go back. When she did, the owner beat her over the head with a pair of grass cutters.[108]

The accounts of attempted escape from Ranong are particularly grim. Three Burmese girls who had attempted to escape from a brothel later raided by police in June 1992 said they were stripped naked and whipped by pimps with steel coat-hangers. Photographs in the Thai newspapers revealed the scars.[109]

Arrest and deportation are not seen as a desirable way of leaving the brothel; the women fear nothing more. Arrest can lead to a new round of extortion and abuse in the Immigration Detention Center in Bangkok; deportation at the border can lead into a new cycle of prostitution on the Thai side or imprisonment on the Burmese side. Thus, most women thus find themselves dependent for their safe return home on the same people who brought them into the brothels. There is a perverse logic in this. The owner and agents have the money to get them back; they know the way and have the police protection to get them there; and they have an interest in getting the girls back so they can recruit their successors.

The demand for "new girls" is continuous, as the young age of most of those we interviewed attests (only two of the thirty women we interviewed were twenty years or older when they first entered the brothels). The clients want girls who are younger and infection-free. For the owners, the naivete of the new girls is a plus, because it enables them to perpetuate their economic control. The result is a constant turnover of girls and women in the brothels, with few of the girls staying in one brothel longer than seven months. When owners have several brothels, they appear to move the girls around every three or four months so there

---

[108] See footnote 87.

[109] "CSD Police Free 36 Girls from Sex-Pit in Ranong," *Bangkok Post,* June 11, 1992.

will be a steady supply of new faces. If a woman can no longer bring in the ten clients a night that make her so profitable for the owner, it is in his interest to move her on or take her back to her village and use her to find a replacement.

Given the desire of all the women and girls we interviewed to return home, it is worth noting again the two cases pointed out earlier in which two women we interviewed had returned to prostitution in Thailand after safely getting back to their villages. Those cases are instructive because they indicate the impact of the brothels on the girls' self-image. Both decided that since they had lost their virginity anyway, there was no point in staying at home; they might as well return to Thailand and try to make more money. Their return to prostitution was voluntary only in the sense that they saw their first experience as having rendered them unfit for anything else.

The women interviewed from brothels in Ranong claimed they were in the brothels much longer than their counterparts in other cities and only when they were sick or sold as wives could they leave. In 1991, three Burmese women from "Myo Myo's" brothel were sold as wives to Thai businessmen for 10,000 baht ($400) each; one woman interviewed named "Kyi Kyi" was hoping to leave the same way in 1992.

For a very fortunate few, local NGO intervention during the raid and arrest at times offered another option of release to an emergency shelter run by a Thai NGO (see Chapter V). But as of mid-1993, those shelters probably served a few hundred women, only a tiny fraction of those trafficked into Thailand.

V. THE THAI GOVERNMENT'S ROLE

As noted in the background section of this report, the Chuan administration pledged in November 1992 to crackdown on forced and child prostitution and trafficking, with particular attention to official complicity in such practices. Our investigation reveals clear official involvement in virtually every stage of the trafficking process yet little concerted effort has been made by the Thai authorities to investigate and punish such abuse by their own agents. This pattern of impunity applies equally to pimps, brothel-owners and recruiters involved in forced prostitution or trafficking.

While the abusers have enjoyed near total impunity, the victims have met with the full force of the law. The Thai government, rather than "rescuing" the women and girls as pledged, is in fact wrongfully arresting them, either as prostitutes or illegal immigrants. Where the Burmese women and girls are concerned, this unlawful arrest inevitably leads to their summary deportation and a range of abuses along the way in violation of both national and international law.

A. OFFICIAL INVOLVEMENT IN TRAFFICKING: A PATTERN OF IMPUNITY[110]

Despite clear national and international prohibitions on procurement and trafficking, such practices are not only widespread in Thailand, but in many instances occur with the direct involvement of Thai police or border guards. Thai border and provincial police control all roads from the Burmese border into Thailand, and several border checkpoints have been set up. It is extremely difficult for Burmese to cross the border and travel any distance without the knowledge and involvement of the Thai police. The brothel agents are well supplied with money to pay them off.

Of the thirty Burmese women and girls we interviewed, ten were willing and able to identify police who had been involved in transporting them from the border into Chiangrai or directly to the brothel.

---

[110] Due to the lack of access to Burma and the minimal information available about what is happening throughout the country, we were unable to ascertain the extent of Burmese official involvement in trafficking. However, testimony from some of the women we interviewed backed by other limited information available suggests knowledge or complicity of Burmese officials.

● "Nu Nu," was brought by an agent to a policeman in Mae Sai. The policeman, complete with uniform, walkie-talkie and gun, then drove "Nu Nu" to Chiangmai.

● "Pyone Pyone" spent three days in Mae Sai at the home of an agent before a uniformed policeman arrived and drove her and twelve other Burmese girls from the agent's house to a brothel in Bangkok. Their van was not stopped at any of the police checkpoints along the way. When she got to the brothel, "Pyone Pyone" was told she could not leave. She said she knew there was no way to escape anyway, because all the police in the area knew the policeman who had brought her there.

● "Thanda" came to Mae Sai when she was seventeen years old, found a job and left for Bangkok all in one day. The police stopped the car en route to Chiangrai and brought everyone to the police station. In the end, the driver had to pay 26,000 baht ($1,040) for "Thanda" because she was an illegal Burmese, and they continued on to the brothel.

Once the women and girls are in the Thai brothels the involvement of the police persists. Brothels routinely operate with police knowledge and often with the benefit of police protection, despite the clear prohibition on such establishments under the Anti-Prostitution Act. A recent CSD raid exemplified the extent of government involvement in the brothels. On July 26, 1993, the CSD raided houses of suspected "call-girls" in Bangkok and arrested eighty-nine girls holding fake Thai identity cards. The police also found account books listing protection payments to Thai government officials (including special police task units, immigration officials and the CSD policemen).[111]

In many instances, brothels are located next door to or down the street from local police stations. For example, a July 1993 raid involving over 148 Burmese women and girls took place on three brothels in Ranong not far from the local immigration detention center. One woman we interviewed, "Thuza," explained to us her inability to escape by the

---

[111] "89 Suspected Call-Girls Arrested," *The Nation*, July 28, 1993.

fact that the police station was just next door. She said it was impossible to leave because the policemen came every day to the brothel, usually in full uniform and carrying guns. Often, they were her clients. They knew all the girls and the brothel owner.

Fifty percent of the Burmese women and girls we interviewed reported having police as clients. Most of those who reported police as clients told of special privileges the police received from the brothel owner.

● "Aye Aye," who came to Thailand when she was fourteen years old, told us that the police came often to the Dao Kanong brothel in Bangkok where she worked. They usually came in uniform in groups of two to five men and were very friendly with the owner. The policemen were the only ones allowed to take girls out of the brothel, and they never had to pay. "Aye Aye" had to go out with policemen on two occasions. Both times the men were in full uniform with walkie-talkies and guns.

● "Nu Nu," the girl who was kept for one year in a back room with other children in the Mekong brothel in Samut Sakhorn, told us she was taken out twice for the whole night by policemen in full uniform with guns and walkie-talkies. The first time, a policeman took her to his house and during the night, other policemen came and had sex with her. The second time she was taken out to a party with two other girls from the brothel where they all served many men throughout the night.

● "Nilar" was fifteen years old when she was brought to a brothel in Thailand. She told us that she saw policemen around the brothel all the time. At least every ten days a group of uniformed policemen would come to see the owner. Sometimes they took girls. Other times they just had tea with the brothel owner. The policemen chose "Nilar" twice. Both were in full uniforms with guns. "Nilar" was afraid that they would arrest her, but both assured her many times that they would not.

● In the case of "Chit Chit," it was a policeman named Bu Muad who brought her to the brothel and raped her en route. He turned out to be the pimp at the Mae Lim brothel in Chiangmai province. "Chit Chit" was arrested once at this brothel and brought to the local police station with fifteen other Burmese girls from the same brothel. The police station was just at the end of the street. The police asked specifically about Bu Muad for two hours. Then, the brothel owner paid 50 baht ($2) for each girl's release, and they all returned to the brothel with the owner the same day. The brothel was closed for one week. Then the policemen came and told the owners they could reopen.

In several cases we investigated, the local police involved in the so-called "rescue" process actually were former clients of the arrested Burmese girls. For example,

● when the police came to arrest "Nu Nu" she recognized one of the policemen as a client of hers in the brothel. In addition, "Nu Nu" recognized three other policemen-clients at the station. For reasons unknown to "Nu Nu" the police did not put her in a cell, but kept her in the police office for three days. "Nu Nu" said the police officers teased her, although not to the point of physical abuse.

● Similarly, on a Saturday night, five police officers "Tar Tar" had never seen came to the brothel, and took "Tar Tar" to the police station. There she recognized some of the policemen at the station as friends of the brothel owner and clients of the women with whom she was arrested.

Frequently, when a woman or girl is arrested, local police then allow brothel owners access to her in custody. The fact that Burmese women usually arrive at the jails with no resources of any kind makes them extremely vulnerable to being trafficked back into brothels. Brokers often visit the local jails offering to pay off the inmates' fines and transportation costs in exchange for labor.

Several of the Burmese we interviewed had previously been arrested by local police and returned to the brothel after the owner paid money to the police. Their fine was then added to their debt and furthered their bondage to the owner. For example,

● When "Sanda" came to Thailand when she was seventeen years old and was arrested one month later in May 1992, she witnessed the brothel owner buy the release of three older women arrested with her.

● When "Aye Aye" was arrested the first time, the brothel owner came to the police station and bought her release.

● When "Chit Chit" was arrested the brothel owner paid the police 50 baht ($2) to release her and she was returned to the brothel.

● When "Yin Yin" was arrested, along with twenty-nine other girls, ten older women and ten men, the brothel owner came and bought out all but thirty girls.

The ad-hoc parliamentary committee that investigated the Songkhla murder (discussed below), found that women and girls arrested in the raids that occurred subsequent to the murder were prosecuted and fined by the Songkhla Court, but instead of being taken to the remand home as required by law, the women were taken back to work by the brothel owners after the fines were paid.[112] Reliable sources report that of the 148 women and girls arrested in a July 14 Ranong raid, fifty-eight were deported to Burma and the rest were released back to brothel owners in Ranong.

Ranong is particularly alarming because of the extent to which the local police and government authorities condone and at times collaborate in systematic abuse of Burmese women and girls. In one article, the Ranong chief inspector Police Lieutenant Colonel Sudchai Yanrat claimed that it would be easy for the police to actively weed out illegal migrants

---

[112] "Songkhla Murder Panel Wants Welfare Officials, Police Probed," *Bangkok Post*, November 11, 1992.

and foreign prostitutes, but such a campaign could ruin the fragile economy of Ranong, which depends strongly on Burmese laborers.[113]

In a similar vein, a Ranong merchant was quoted in the same article as saying,

> ...anyone who hopes to win a seat as Ranong's MP must publicly announce a clear policy supporting border trade.... and that means easing restrictions on illegal migrant labor, and on foreign prostitutes.[114]

The Songkhla Murder

The extent of official involvement in protecting the brothel owners' interests was graphically exposed by the murder in Songkhla province of Passawara Samrit, a Thai woman from Chiangmai. Her murder was discovered on November 2, 1992, the same day Prime Minister Chuan Leekpai announced his nationwide crackdown on child and forced prostitution. According to witnesses, Passawara was caught planning an escape from the brothel and received death threats from both the owner and police officers who frequented the brothel. She fled on November 1 to the provincial hospital seeking help; the staff turned her over to the welfare department at the Songkhla provincial hall. The welfare office concluded that she should be turned over to the local police because of inconsistencies in her account. At the end of the day, while still at the welfare office, Passawara went to the bathroom and never returned. The next morning, her body was found with her throat slashed.[115]

On December 1, Songkhla police investigating the murder announced that six suspects had been charged: two provincial officers, two police, the

---

[113] "Ranong's 'Constructive Engagement' Poses Big Dilemma," *Bangkok Post*, September 13, 1992.

[114] Ibid.

[115] "Mystery Surrounds the Death of a Prostitute in Songkhla," *Bangkok Post*, November 8, 1992.

son-in-law of the brothel owner and a pimp.[116] The investigation revealed that two police officers to whom Passawara initially turned for assistance had tried to convince her to return to the brothel and work off her "debt" to the owner. These officers reportedly threatened to arrest her for prostitution if she refused to return.[117] An independent inquiry conducted by an ad hoc committee of the lower house of the Thai parliament, found that the police station implicated in the case had received payoffs from the brothel owner involved.[118]

Following the investigation, twenty Songkhla policemen were reportedly transferred. The transfer announced by the Provincial Police Commissioner of Bureau 4, was said not to be related to the death of Passawara Samrit, but rather to the officers' poor performance, idleness and willingness to allow "bad incidents to occur."[119] One sergeant was also charged with taking bribes from the brothel owner.

In a tacit admission of police involvement in or, at a minimum, tolerance of prostitution, Assistant Police Chief Pracha Prommok told southern police officers in the wake of the Songkhla murder to "suppress prostitution in areas under their jurisdiction." He warned that policemen discovered accepting kickbacks will face tough and punitive action."[120] Pracha also ordered southern police to make maps of all the illegal brothels operating in their areas and warned that if child or forced prostitution were found in any area, chief police officers would be punished.[121]

However, despite this clear prohibition on police involvement, with the exception of the Songkhla case, not a single Thai police officer has

---

[116] "Police Have Strong Evidence in Prostitute Murder Case," *Bangkok Post*, December 2, 1992.

[117] "Renewing the Debate on Legalizing Prostitution," *The Nation*, November 6, 1992.

[118] "Songkhla Police Face Transfer," *The Nation*, January 30, 1993.

[119] "20 Songkhla Policemen Transferred," *The Nation*, March 9, 1993.

[120] "Chavalit Wants All Brothels Closed," *Bangkok Post*, November 7, 1992.

[121] Ibid.

been charged or prosecuted for such activities. In a September 1993 interview, Prime Minister Chuan again acknowledged the continuing role of "immorality and negligence by government officials" in obstructing the effort to suppress prostitution.[122] Police Major General Bancha Netinan indicated that the police department was "cracking down on staff involvement of the flesh trade."[123] He told reporters that 302 inactive posts had been prepared for police officials found to be involved in prostitution. While any improvement in efforts to curtail official involvement in child and forced prostitution is welcome, the transfer of guilty officers is no substitute for the prosecution and punishment of state agents involved in such abuse.

B. NON-ARREST OF TRAFFICKERS, PIMPS, PROCURERS, BROTHEL OWNERS AND CLIENTS

This pattern of impunity also applies to brothel owners, pimps and recruiters whom the police and courts have largely exempted from arrest or punishment. Several of the known brothel raids occurring in 1991, 1992 and early 1993 did involve the arrest of pimps and brothel owners, but these efforts have been extremely limited. For example, the June 1992 raid involving thirty-three Burmese women and girls brought in two guards and two members of the brothel owners' family, but the brothel owner escaped. The July 1992 raid on five Ranong brothels involving seventy-nine Burmese women and girls netted two brothel owners, but the others escaped. According to news reports, a July 8, 1993 raid in the Muang District of Kanchanaburi involved the arrest of thirty-two Burmese women and girls, but the pimps and brothel owner escaped.[124] Impunity for all but the women appears to be the rule rather than the exception.

- When "Moe Moe" was nineteen years old she was arrested

---

[122] "Chuan Declares All-Out War on Child Prostitution," *The Nation*, September 28, 1993.

[123] Ibid.

[124] "Police save 79 Burmese Women from Five Brothels," *The Nation*, July 9, 1992.

along with twenty-seven other girls and women. The brothel owner was not arrested, while a man working at a front counter was initially arrested but later released. "Moe Moe" was sent to a detention center in Bangkok.

● "Yin Yin" was arrested along with twenty-nine other women and girls and ten men working in the brothel. The ten men were later released, but the girls were sent to a detention center in Bangkok. The brothel owner was not arrested.

● "Phyu Phyu" was arrested with six other girls also working in the brothel; the owner was not. Plainclothes policemen blocked all the doors and only allowed the men out. The clients were asked by police to go and "come back another day." The brothel owner was not arrested.

In those few instances where agents, pimps or brothel owners have been arrested, they have routinely been charged under the Act for the Abatement of Prostitution which carries lesser penalties than those provided under the Penal Code.[125]

In only one known instance has a brothel owner been charged under the Penal Code. In 1984 a fire broke out in the brothel area near Phuket island south of Thailand. Five women were burned in the fire as they were chained in a room and unable to escape. Charges were filed against the brothel owners under the penal code and the trial lasted for approximately seven years. Eventually, the families of the victims were compensated and the brothel owners imprisoned.[126]

In general, however, the prosecution of brothel owners, whether under the penal or anti-prostitution law, is virtually non-existent. In an interview with us on March 4, Colonel Surasak pointed out that in

---

[125] Vitit Muntarbhorn, "A Scourge in Our Midst," *Bangkok Post*, November 13, 1992.

[126] Anchana Suvarananda, "Traffic in Women in Thailand," in *Traffic in Women: Violation of Women's Dignity and Fundamental Human Rights*, Asian Women's Human Rights Council, 1993, p. 158-173.

holding the brothel owners accountable,

> it is not just a matter of revising the prostitution law and
> pressuring the police to implement it. There must also be
> pressure on the judicial system to prosecute the cases and
> not allow them to settle out of court. Many times the
> investigation is intentionally obstructed. The judges must
> sentence, not just let [the accused brothel owners] off
> with a fine.

In a subsequent press interview on April 1, Surasak expanded on
his remarks, noting that the Anti-Prostitution law was full of loopholes
that benefit the sex-traders. He told reporters,

> The fine is too light. The existing laws are quite out of
> date. It's true that the brothel owners just resume the
> business as there's no order from the judges to close their
> seedy operations.[127]

Brothel owners not only escape punishment for procurement and
brothel operation, but also for the range of abuses committed in the
course of these illicit practices. Debt bondage, illegal confinement, forced
labor, and negligence are commonly committed against Burmese women
and girls, and others, in Thailand's brothels in clear violation of
international and national law. Yet, to our knowledge, not a single
brothel owner has ever been investigated or punished for such abuses.
Similarly, clients who engage in the statutory rape of underage girls in
the brothels have never been sanctioned, despite the clear prohibition in
the Penal Code on sex with girls under the age of fifteen. Nor have
brothel owners been punished for aiding and abetting this offense.

C. DISCRIMINATORY AND ARBITRARY ARREST OF TRAFFICKING VICTIMS

While the Chuan administration has failed to arrest the largely male
state agents, brothel owners, pimps, recruiters and clients involved in

---

[127] "Chuan's War On Sexploitation Seen as a Failure," *Bangkok Post*, April 2,
1993.

forced prostitution, trafficking and associated violations, it has engaged in a routine practice of arresting female victims of such abuse. This constitutes a clear violation of the Thai government's obligations under CEDAW. In ratifying the Convention, which it did in August 1985, Thailand agreed "To take all appropriate measures, including legislation, to modify or abolish existing laws, regulations, customs and practices which constitute discrimination against women," and to "accord to women equality with men before the law."[128]

To some extent, this discrimination is imbedded in Thai domestic law. As noted in the background section above, the Anti-Prostitution law penalizes prostitutes, who are predominately female, but exempts their male clients. The law clearly prohibits female "promiscuity" -- and seeks to "reform" such behavior -- while tolerating similar behavior in males and making no provision whatsoever for their reform. However, even where the law is neutral on its face, as in the case of the provisions that penalize both prostitution and procurement, it is applied by the Thai authorities in a discriminatory manner resulting in the arrest of female prostitutes but impunity for their predominately male agents, pimps, brothel owners and clients.

This discriminatory arrest pattern is rendered that much more egregious by the fact that the vast majority of the women and girls should never have been arrested in the first place. Thailand's Anti-Trafficking law explicitly exempts trafficking victims -- unlike others in the country illegally -- from imprisonment and fines. The government has simply chosen not to apply this law. As a result, the Burmese women and girls have been caught up in the crackdown and wrongfully arrested either as illegal immigrants under the Immigration Act, or as prostitutes. This practice not only abrogates the minimal protection available under the Anti-Trafficking law, but also is contrary to international norms in this regard, which call on states to make "suitable provisions for [trafficking victims'] temporary care and maintenance."[129]

---

[128] Convention on the Elimination of All Forms of Discrimination Against Women, Part I, Article 2, and Part IV, Article 15.

[129] It is also contrary to the Thai government's own efforts on behalf of Thai women trafficked to Japan and subsequently arrested as illegal immigrants. When the Japanese government indicated in July 1993 that it planned a crackdown on illegal immigrants in August, Thai officials urged Japan to "waive the use of jail

Thailand's Anti-Trafficking law also requires Thai authorities to arrange and shoulder the cost of the victims' repatriation to their country of origin. These provisions are consistent with the International Convention on the Suppression of Traffic in Persons and the Exploitation of the Prostitution of Others (the Trafficking Convention) which calls for the delay of repatriation until "agreement is reached with the country of origin,"[130] the expense of which should be borne by the host government. Thai authorities, however, routinely ignore these provisions. Under the Chuan administration, arrest for illegal immigration has become more commonplace, resulting in the detention and summary deportation of women and girls, usually at their own expense.

D. VIOLATIONS OF DUE PROCESS

The arrest of the Burmese women and girls as prostitutes, or more routinely, as illegal immigrants is not only discriminatory and without sound legal justification, but also is frequently carried out in clear violation of basic principles of due process as provided both in international norms and in Thailand's Criminal Procedure Code. Even the minimal due process protection provided in the Immigration Act is regularly ignored.

International law sets forth a variety of due process protection for persons who have been arrested or detained. These principles are set forth in a number of instruments, including the International Covenant on Civil and Political Rights (ICCPR) and the Body of Principles for the Protection of All Persons under Any Form of Detention or Imprisonment (Body of Principles), which was adopted by the U.N. General Assembly in 1988. While Thailand has not yet acceded to the ICCPR, its provisions,

---

as a punishment for all Thais facing arrest and secure reliable measures to protect Thai women from harassment by their Japanese gangster bosses." Kyodo News Service, July 27, 1993 in Foreign Broadcast Information Service FBIS-EAS-93-143, July 28, 1993, p.78. Thailand also urged Japan to pay all repatriation costs and form a "repatriation committee" to arrange the workers' safe return to Thailand.

[130] The Convention on the Suppression of the Traffic in Persons and the Exploitation of the Prostitution of Others, Article 19, March 21, 1950.

like those contained in the Body of Principles, establish an internationally recognized framework for examining due process protection.

The Body of Principles provides a number of due process protections relevant to the arbitrary arrest of the Burmese women and girls. First, it provides that anyone who is arrested must be informed upon arrest of the reasons for the arrest and be promptly informed of the charges against her. Upon arrest and detention, all persons must be provided by the responsible authority with an explanation of her rights and how to avail herself of those rights. A person who does not fully understand or speak the language used by the authorities is entitled to promptly receive the information mentioned in a language she understands.[131]

In the case of the Burmese women and girls these principles appear to be honored more in the breach than the observance. The CSD and their local police partners appear unable to establish a consistent rationale for the arrests and, to our knowledge, they often conduct them without warrant. Children and foreigners appear to be the primary targets for "rescue," but in some raids, the police took only the girls or women whom they had identified by name, sometimes acting at the request of family members or NGOs. In others, all those who were under eighteen years or in immediate need of health care were removed, and in some raids, every female in the brothel was arrested. Older Thai women caught in the raids are usually released or sent to Pakkret. The decision appears entirely to depend on the whim of the CSD and other police units involved.

Some attempts have been made -- due largely to the insistence of local NGOs -- to protect child prostitutes at a minimum from arbitrary arrest. NGOs do appear on occasion to be able to negotiate their participation in certain raids and the release of child prostitutes into their care, but the NGOs presence at raids is not guaranteed and takes place only on an ad-hoc basis.

The arrests themselves do not appear to follow any prescribed procedure. In some instances the girls and women arrested are allowed to gather their belongings before being taken to the police station. However, none of those we interviewed were so fortunate. Many told us

---

[131] Principles 10, 11, 13 and 14 of *Body of Principles for the Protection of All Persons under Any Form of Detention or Imprisonment*, U.N. General Assembly Resolution 43/173 of 9 December 1988.

of being hauled off with only the clothes on their backs. In most instances, they were forced to leave behind not only belongings, but also money owed to them by the brothel owner or meager savings that would later have proved useful, if not essential, to a safe and speedy return to Burma.

> • When "Aye Aye" was arrested, she was not allowed to get any of the belongings she had collected in the brothel over the past four years. "Aye Aye" believed the owner owed her over 30,000 baht ($1,200), although she had never been able to discuss her accounts.

> • "Yin Yin" was arrested by plainclothes policemen along with twenty-nine women and ten men working at the brothel. She lost all of her belongings in the arrest. "Yin Yin" had kept her valuables with the owner and could not get them back, even when she later met the owner at the police station to which she was brought.

CSD officials and other individuals involved in the raids told us that the haste in which raids are carried out results from the need to get the girls away from the brothel quickly before the owner or local police involved with the brothels operations have time to intervene. Nonetheless, in an interview with us in March 1993, the CSD Police Colonel Surasak Suttharom acknowledged that preventing the women from collecting their personal effects was both unnecessarily punitive and risked further profiting the brothel owner.

All those arrested in police raids are taken to local police stations. Some are subsequently released to NGO shelters, but the majority are taken to police lock-ups. The Burmese women and girls we interviewed reported major inconsistencies in the procedures followed by the authorities with regard to where and how they were detained; if and how they were charged; if they were tried; the fine and length of sentence; and the procedure followed for their release or deportation. The arresting officer appears to have unlimited discretion to decide these questions, despite clear procedural guidelines to the contrary.

The Thai Criminal Procedure Code provides that "... the officer making the arrest shall notify the person to be arrested that he is under arrest." Yet, without exception, the girls and women we interviewed claimed that when arrested they were given no explanation of their rights by the police.

Many of the women and girls told us that once arrested they were not informed of the charges against them. This constitutes not only a direct violation of the Body of Principles but also of the Thai Criminal Procedure Code which obligates arresting officials immediately to take the person to the office of an administrative or police official and "notify him of the cause of the arrest."[132] While in some instances, our interviewees reported that official procedures were followed, they told us that questions were routinely put to them in Thai and they frequently did not understand what was being said or decided. Often they were given papers to sign which they could not read.

Most of the women and girls were asked only their name, age and address by the police. Not a single women or girl we interviewed reported being given an opportunity to explain how she came to Thailand, what abuses she suffered in the brothels or what fears she might have in returning to Burma. It is under these circumstances that they were held pending deportation.

E. PROLONGED DETENTION, SUMMARY TRIALS AND CUSTODIAL ABUSE

The Body of Principles for the Protection of All Persons Under Any Form of Detention or Imprisonment requires that persons who are detained must be allowed an effective opportunity to be heard promptly before a judge or other authority and be given the opportunity to defend themselves. A detained person is entitled to legal counsel and must be permitted to consult with her counsel. In addition, both the Criminal Procedure Code and Immigration Act clearly prohibit the holding of detainees for over forty-eight hours, unless necessitated by the investigation or other exigencies. In no circumstances is detention for over seven days allowed without permission from the court.[133]

Yet many of the women and girls we interviewed who were taken to the local police stations, immigration detention centers or reform homes report being held, often for several days and in some instances for

---

[132] Criminal Procedure Code of Thailand, 1957, section 84.

[133] Criminal Procedure Code, Section 87 and Immigration Act, section 20.

months, without any judicial hearing or access to counsel.

One Burmese woman we interviewed, "Htet Htet," found herself in prolonged detention in a series of local jails in Thailand one day after having been kidnapped by a brothel agent in Burma.

> • Upon arrival at the brothel, "Htet Htet" was arrested with six other Burmese. The couple who owned the brothel and two men who worked with them also were arrested. They were all brought to the Prachinburi police station (about two hours northeast of Bangkok). The couple and two men were released the same morning. The police asked the Burmese their names and ages but no questions about the brothel or conditions there. She was kept with the five other Burmese girls and women in the local Prachinburi police station for two months before being taken further east to Aranyaprathet.[134] There they were jailed for another twenty days, whereupon "Htet Htet" was sent to Kanchanaburi police station, seven hours west of Aranyaprathet. She stayed in the local jail for one week before being deported across the Thai-Burmese border.

During our visit to the IDC in Bangkok in January 1993, "Nan Li Li" had been detained for over eight months. "Nan Li Li" had stayed in a local police station in Songkhla for three months and then was transferred to the IDC in Bangkok where she remained for the next five months. The other inmates reported that she had gone "crazy" and just kept saying over and over again that she only wanted to go home via Mae Sai. The transportation fee to Mae Sai, however, was 3,000 baht ($120), and she had no money.

Most of the women and girls we interviewed in the penal reform institution, Pakkret, had been there for anywhere from one to six months without ever being charged, appearing before a judge or having the benefit of counsel. In the course of their detention in these various institutions, the women and girls uniformly reported custodial abuse and ill-treatment and abusive prison conditions.

---

[134] Aranyaprathet is due east of Bangkok along the Thai-Cambodian border.

Local Jails

In the course of being arrested and deported, the Burmese girls and women reported being kept in overcrowded jails without any regard to age, circumstance of arrest or status in the judicial process. None of the girls or women were ever officially allowed out for exercise, but reported being called out to wash dishes or provide other "favors" to the police which often involved sexual harassment and abuse. Inmates received no explanation of the rules in the jails, but according to those interviewed, infractions were punished by beatings. Several of the Burmese interviewed spoke of writings on the jail walls, warning women of incidents of rape by police of female inmates. They reported that no female officers or guards were accessible to female inmates.

Immigration Detention Center (IDC)

At the IDC, the detainees are held in conditions which fall far short of the U.N Standard Minimum Rules for the Treatment of Prisoners. They are also subject to extortion and physical abuse. The IDC, located on Suan Phlu street in central Bangkok, consists of eight cells, each 60' x 25', with between 150 and 200 inmates in each cell. Six of the cells are for men, and two are for women and children. With the exception of a few beds in the women's cell reserved for "room leaders" (women used by immigration officers to control other inmates), all inmates sleep on the floor so close together they cannot roll over. Sometimes, they must take turns lying down. There are small windows at the top of the cell only for ventilation, not sunlight. There is one bathroom per cell with six toilets and a small space for a shower. Water is provided only for seven hours a day. The inmates receive two meals a day and no blankets, mats or mosquito nets or other supplies unless someone from the outside brings them in for them. From the day they are detained at the IDC until the day they are deported, inmates are not allowed to leave the room. Visitors and NGO staff who visit the jail are the only link between inmates and the outside world.[135]

---

[135] Visitors with passports or Thai ID are allowed in Monday through Friday for two hours each morning. They have their bags and pockets checked upon entering the IDC, and it is up to the guard what will be allowed in. All conversations are with inmates while in their cell and are monitored by "room

An extensive underworld run by the room leaders pervades the IDC. The room leaders, themselves illegal immigrants, are extremely powerful and feared and operate in both female and male cells. They have a collaborative relationship with the officials to handle the necessary "cleaning" and transportation fees and other business transactions. The latter includes purchasing of coffee, food and drugs as well as selling and buying of release papers among inmates. Inmates often ask visitors not to come to the detention center because room leaders (and immigration officers), knowing they have a connection with the outside, usually put more pressure on them to "share" or pay more money for transport fees and other bribes. The room leaders in the women's cells are well dressed, with fancy barrettes, make-up and fingernail polish. Although we do not have direct evidence, many of the women and girls we interviewed told us that prostitution inside the detention center is common. We noted that the appearance of several of the women and girls in the detention indicated that they had some independent income, despite the fact that many had been detained up to ten months.[136]

There are also frequent reports of sexual harassment and beatings by immigration officers, guards and police associated with the IDC. However, such abuse is difficult to document because no private conversation is allowed in the IDC nor is it possible for inmates to report an incident of police abuse. There are no female guards or officers assigned to the women's cell.

> ● "Muyar" was twenty-three years old when she was
> arrested and her experience is typical of the women and
> girls detained in the IDC. When she first arrived at the
> IDC she was fingerprinted and then sent to a cell

---

leaders", putting the inmate in an extremely difficult position to talk openly.

[136] There are both immigration officers and guards, hired by the Ministry of Interior (MOI), working in the IDC. The guards are not responsible to the Immigration officers in charge of the jail and their superiors are located far from the IDC. The guards are known to be very involved in the underworld of the IDC, and immigration officers turn a blind eye. However, they also have their own rackets which usually revolve around the bribes and fees for deportation. Both the MOI and Immigration office operate independently and each tends to blame the other when confronted with corruption.

number seven where she spent the next forty-two days. She saw many incidents of sexual harassment of female inmates by IDC officials. For example, each day when the food was delivered, an officer would point to who was to come to collect and distribute the meal. He would then touch and do whatever he wanted to her in front of everyone. The women also complained to each other of policemen "using" them when they went to get fingerprinted, questioned or photographed. The second time "Muyar" was fingerprinted, she was taken out of the cell with about twenty other girls and women. Two Burmese and one Chinese girl were taken aside and in front of the others, several policemen grabbed their breasts and touched their bodies. They did this while calling out the names of the other girls and women who were to come forward. If they hesitated, they would be hit hard with a stick. "Muyar" said it was terrible for those who did not understand Thai and did not hear when their name or number was called. After everyone was fingerprinted, they were returned to the cell.

Another incident, documented by a local NGO, illustrates the vulnerability to abuse of women detainees.

● K, T, and P were three women of the Karen ethnic group, all about seventeen years old, who found themselves in the Immigration Detention Center in Bangkok in December 1991. K and T had been trafficked into prostitution, tried to escape and had been arrested as illegal immigrants; P had been a market trader, also arrested for illegal entry. On December 9, they were transferred to the IDC in Kanchanaburi, together with seven men, for eventual deportation. On December 22, they were taken out of the prison by truck to Sangkhlaburi town, where the women were transferred to a private pick-up truck and driven around the town three times, "as if being paraded", according to one observer. They were then taken to the house of the assistant district officer (*palaat*). A Karen man, who had followed the truck out of concern for the women, spoke with a Thai police officer at the *palaat*'s house. The policeman said that both women and men deportees were being conscripted to work for one day on the Three Pagodas Pass Festival, under the supervision of the Burmese civilian militia, the Aw Daw. The police officer then accompanied the women from the house to Three Pagodas Pass (on the Burmese side of the border), about a half hour away. When they arrived, at a barracks-like building (the nature of which is unclear from the account) divided into rooms for male and female conscripts, they were told to take showers, which they did with the local militia watching. The Thai policeman then told K to come to his room for questioning. She did so, and when she was inside, he locked the door and told her to sit on the bed. When she said she preferred to stand, he grabbed her and tried to force her on to the bed, slapping her on the face and arms as he did so. She managed to get out of his grasp, unlock the door and get outside. T and P heard her screams and rushed to help her. After this incident, the three women had to cook for all the conscripts involved in the Festival until December 26, when one Karen conscript pointed the women out to friends living in Three Pagodas Pass. They managed to pull the women away and get them to safety back on the Thai side of the border.

The Penal Reform Institutions

Most of the women and girls we interviewed had been detained in the penal reform institution of Pakkret. Most referred to Pakkret as a prison. They resented the harsh restrictions imposed on them, many of which they did not understand. All communication with the outside world was monitored, with strict limitations on contacts with the outside world. Each day was tightly scheduled with training in domestic skills, including sewing and cooking. No cosmetics were allowed, and smoking was banned.

According to the women and girls we interviewed, the Pakkret wardens carried out a kind of disciplinary surveillance. The disciplinary measures included public humiliation and/or beatings. The Burmese were housed in separate quarters from the Thai women and wore different colored uniforms: the Burmese women and girls dressed in purple, while the Thai women and girls wore blue.

● "Tar Tar," found Pakkret too strict and considered it a jail. She told us that all the mail coming in or going out was opened, and that inmates were not allowed to use the phone. The girls were hit often because they did not know all the rules. They were even beaten for talking while eating. Usually the matrons noted down all their misdeeds, and in the evening, the dorm leader would beat the offenders in front of everyone else. During the day, the inmates wore uniforms so they could not run away and badges to identify their dormitory. The dorm rooms, according to "Tar Tar", were locked from the outside at night by three doors.

Some women and girls in Pakkret have attempted to escape from the reformatory. In one case, a Burmese girl named "Than Than" told us, the attempt ended in death.

● "Than Than," said her friend, Mai Jai Ngam, drowned trying to escape. When Mai had first arrived at Pakkret, she was told she must turn over her gold necklace. She did not do so, and later, a matron saw the necklace and took it from her. Mai accused her of stealing, but the head matron accused Mai herself of lying after the alleged thief denied having taken the necklace. The matron warned Mai that she might have to stay at Pakkret for ten years, according to "Than Than." That evening, at 6 P.M. when the dinner bell rang, Mai Jai Ngam was not among the rest of the girls. The matron went to look for her and saw her on the pier. As staff went to get her, "Than Than" saw Mai Jai Ngam jump into the river. Three days later her body was found downstream near a temple.

Women can also apparently be sent back to brothels from the

reform houses. Once a warden was caught red-handed sending some of the inmates back to the brothel.[137]

> ● "Tar Tar" told us that after she had been in Pakkret for four months, three policemen and one police woman, all in uniform, came to get "Buang Bao", a Burmese woman from Keng Tung, a Burmese town north of the Thai-Burmese border. "Buang Bao" told "Tar Tar" that she could see the owner of the brothel she had worked for on the other side of the pier, and pointed him out to "Tar Tar" as she left. "Tar Tar" then saw the police hand "Buang Bao" over to the owner. Before "Buang Bao" left, she gave "Tar Tar" the address of the brothel she worked at if she ever wanted a job.

One of the most disturbing elements of the reports of arbitrary detention, poor conditions and ill-treatment in Pakkret is that Thai authorities have blocked all outside efforts to investigate or monitor conditions there. NGOs are simply denied access.

Lack of Fair Trials

Most of the women and girls we interviewed were subjected to prolonged detention, often in abusive conditions, without trial in clear violation of Thai law and international principles of due process.

If any person is charged as a prostitute, the Anti-Prostitution law requires that she or he be tried in a court of law. The Criminal Procedure Code requires that in court "the charge be read out and explained to the accused."[138] If found guilty, the accused must, under the Anti-Prostitution law, be imprisoned or fined and remanded to a penal reform institution.

Under the Anti-Trafficking law, trials also are required for the women and girls, but no fines or imprisonment are set forth. The law does require that the women be sent to a reform institution for thirty days, prior to the arrangement of their deportation by Thai authorities.

---

[137] Ibid.

[138] Criminal Procedure Code, section 172.

This thirty-day period may be extended, but only by judicial order. This law, although it needs amending, should have been applied to the Burmese women and girls caught in the crackdown. If it had been, a judicial order would have been required to obtain and/or extend the detention of the Burmese women and girls in Pakkret. As noted, the women and girls we interviewed never saw a judge and the majority were detained in Pakkret from three to six months.

Our lack of access to the local jails or to Pakkret made it difficult to determine the degree to which those women and girls arrested for prostitution were actually tried before being imprisoned or sent to reform institutions. Only one Burmese girl we interviewed, "Soe Soe" aged seventeen, spoke of being taken before a judge after four days in detention in a local police station in Bang Na.

For those Burmese women and girls who are arrested under the Immigration Act, the requirements for trial and judicial oversight appear to be minimal. The Immigration Act itself provides that in the case where an alien with prohibited characteristics, including "having behaved in a manner that is believed to have engaged in prostitution," a competent officer "can issue a written order for such an alien to leave the Kingdom."[139] No trial is required, although aliens in this category are granted rights to appeal with the exception of those who entered the country without a passport or visa, or who were barred entry by the Minister of Immigration "for the benefit of the country" or other similar state interests.[140]

To our knowledge, and without access to the local jails or the IDCs this is difficult to determine with certainty, while deportation orders may be issued, Burmese women and girls have not enjoyed the right of appeal. In instances where hearings do occur, they are

---

[139] Immigration Act, 1979, section 22.

[140] Section 22 also provides that "if such an alien is dissatisfied with the order, he may file an appeal against such order with the minister....But if the Minister has not issued an order within seven days of the appeal, it shall be regarded that the Minister issued the order that such an alien is not a person to be prohibited from entering the country....For appeal it must be submitted to the competent officer within forty-eight hours from the time of the receipt of the order from the competent officer and the appeal shall be filed according to the form and rate of fee paid as prescribed in the Ministerial regulations."

characterized by violations of due process.

According not only to the women and girls we interviewed, but to others who have been processed through the IDC, a trial at the IDC is typically held within ten days of a detainee's arrival, in a proceeding where the Burmese have neither legal counsel nor interpreters. The fines for illegally entering the country range from approximately 2,800 baht ($112) or forty days in jail to 4,900 baht ($196) or seventy days in jail.[141]

They often are sentenced without understanding the process and told to sign a form in Thai which they cannot read. If the defendants try to speak at all, they fear they will be considered "difficult" and can receive harsher sentences.

The detention of those held in the IDC is often arbitrarily prolonged by the fact that illegal Burmese immigrants rarely have the resources to pay fines and transport to the border for deportation, an expense amounting to 200 baht ($8). Thus, they must stay in the IDC to pay off the expense at a rate of seventy baht ($2.80) a day.[142]

> ● "Maw Maw" was nineteen years old when she was tried the day after she was arrested. She said she thought the sentence was 4,000 baht ($160) or two months in jail, but she could not understand Thai. She had 500 baht ($20) with her when she was arrested, which was not enough to pay the fine. She was then brought to the IDC, where she stayed for one and a half months.

> ● "Soe Soe" was seventeen years old when she was arrested as an illegal Burmese in Bangkok. She was taken with others to the Bangna Police Station where she stayed for five days. On the fourth day she was fingerprinted and brought to a court. She was told she had to pay 2,000 baht ($80) in order to be sent directly to the IDC. She and the others could not pay and were sent to work in a prison first to earn money. The prison

---

[141] Based on Asia Watch interviews with illegal Burmese immigrants in the Bangkok IDC during 1992-1993.

[142] Ibid.

was three hours outside of Bangkok, but she did not know the name and could not speak Thai. "Soe Soe" was imprisoned there for twenty-five days. Men and women were separated. The men made light bulbs and the women plastic flowers. There were about forty to fifty women there, aged fifteen to thirty. They stayed in a dormitory, not really like a prison. Most of the people there were Thais, most on drug or prostitution charges. The room leader of "Soe Soe" was a Burmese sentenced for two years. They worked from 8 A.M. to noon, 1:00 P.M. to 3:00 P.M. and again from 5:00 P.M. to 8:00 P.M. The room leader often kicked those who would not work or work fast enough. The police she saw there wore tan uniforms. Afterwards, she was returned to the Bang Na police station for eighteen days and then transferred to the IDC. She spent five days in the IDC in Bangkok and one week in the Kanchanaburi IDC before being deported back to Burma.

In addition to the fines and the deportation costs, inmates can be told to pay numerous "fees" to get themselves and their papers through the bureaucracy. For example, inmates spoke to us of being asked to pay for "cleaning fees," documentation expenses (for photographs or photocopies, for example), and transportation costs. In some instances, inmates with release papers, but without the required transportation fees, sell their release papers and identity paper to other inmates for extra cash in the hopes that they can later buy a name and pay the necessary transport fees. Without identification, such individuals get "lost" in the IDC and find themselves detained for years without any opportunity to leave the cell.[143] Although the NGOs try to help by paying the transportation costs to the deportation point, it often happens that the more the inmates pay, the more the officials demand from them.

There are many girls and women in the IDC in Bangkok whose "fines" and transportation costs are negotiated and paid by the brothel

---

[143] This is especially true for nationals whose country of origin does not border Thailand and who must purchase airplane tickets in order to return home. As a result, many try to convince the immigration officials they are Burmese.

owner. The inmate is then released by the police directly to the brothel owner. Amnesty International documented a case in March 1991 when "police tried to force three female Burmese detainees to return to a brothel where they had been made to work as prostitutes. The brothel owner had come to pay fines for their release, but the women refused to go with him." The report then details the violence by police against these three women and another inmate who tried to intervene on the women's behalf.[144]

When we visited the IDC in September 1992, six Burmese women had just been "released to guarantors." Other inmates did not know where the six went and claimed the women themselves were not sure how much they trusted the broker and were uncertain what would happen to them.

Emergency Shelters

NGOs, most of them Thai, have established roughly a dozen shelters which can house women and children who have been released from brothels or local police stations. The ability of the NGOs to intervene is limited, but they are often able to provide temporary protection and a safe haven for those in need of emergency assistance or special protection. The shelters have been able to serve only a few hundred Burmese over the past two years.

The Burmese caseload adds a great strain on already stretched resources of NGOs and has raised many new issues and needs that NGOs are clearly struggling to address. In addition to health care, daily living expenses, counseling and training, the Burmese women need interpreters both in language and culture. Most of those coming from the brothels are HIV positive, raising questions about how they should be educated about AIDS and HIV status in the context of the lack of health care in Burma and their likely reception isolated villages. There is also the question of how NGOs can help them can return home, when the women have no identity cards or travel documents, and when they are, as prostitutes and/or illegal immigrants, considered illegal both in Thailand and Burma, and when they must evade an extensive trafficking network, with unscrupulous brothel owners in league with police.

---

[144] Amnesty International, *"Thailand - Concerns about Treatment of Burmese Refugees,"* ASA 39/15/91 (London: Amnesty International, August 1991)

In addition, the Thai government, in an effort to curb immigration, continues to remind Thai citizens and foreigners in Thailand of the criminal offense of sheltering illegal Burmese. Infringements can entail fines of up to 50,000 baht ($2,000) and imprisonment with a maximum of five years.[145]   Enforcement is arbitrary and does not extend to brothel owners who house the women and girls, but the threat of such penalties makes intervention on behalf of the Burmese women and girls risky for many who would otherwise offer to help.

F. DEPORTATION

Going home is the greatest hope of most of the Burmese women and girls we interviewed, but deportation as illegal immigrants is one of their greatest fears. Both Thai law and international anti-trafficking norms establish mechanisms by which trafficking victims can return to their country of origin without any menace of penalty from either government.   Unfortunately, under the Chuan administration and its predecessor, summary deportation of the women and girls has been the rule, and the process is as corrupt and abusive as every other aspect of the women's and girl's ordeal.

Summary Deportation: The Thai Side

Illegal immigrants, under the Immigration Act of 1979, are responsible for paying the expenses of transport to the border for deportation.[146] The wording of the law suggests they have some choice

---

[145] "PM Orders Arrest of Illegals," *Bangkok Post*, April 11, 1993.

[146] Section 56, Immigration Act of 1979: "Any expenses incurred on repatriation of an alien shall be borne by the owner of a conveyance or person in charge of a conveyance. In the case where an owner or person in charge of a conveyance is not apparent, the offender...shall be required to bear such expenses. In this case, the competent officer has the power to demand the entire expenses in repatriating the alien from any individual offender or collectively as appropriate, but if such alien is asking to leave by any other conveyance or by another route, the alien shall have to bear such expenses himself and therefore may have the approval of the competent officer."

in where they are deported, if they are willing to pay the price. But the scope for extortion is obvious, and the highest prices are often charged for the nearest point of deportation from Bangkok -- Kanchanaburi Province -- because it is easiest to evade SLORC authorities there. Burmese generally prefer to be return to minority-controlled or disputed territories in war zones, and are willing to pay exorbitant amounts to be taken to such areas.

The actual deportation can occur at any of several border crossings overseen by the Ministry of the Interior. The most feared points of deportation are Ranong, Mae Sot, and Mae Sai because of the close collaboration between local Thai and Burmese officials, and because these towns were the point of entry into Thailand for most of the women. Although overall figures on deportation were not available to us at the time of publication, even a casual scrutiny of the Thai press confirms that hundreds of people are deported from Thailand every week.

On July 24, 1993, for example, the *Nation*, the Bangkok English-language daily, reported a round-up of 121 Burmese found working illegally in Muang district in the southern province of Tak. (Some 500 Burmese cross into Tak daily, according to Thai immigration officials.) They were sent to a holding center in Mae Sot, interrogated and quickly deported.

In an earlier incident in July, Tak district officials arrested 131 illegal Burmese immigrants in their province and sent them to a holding center at Ban Dong Pa Kiat for fast deportation. The police official there, Lieutenant Colonel Kriangyut, said his office had arrested six hundred other Burmese in June. They had to be deported immediately because there was no room to detain them and no money to feed them. Cells at police stations throughout the district were so crowded with Burmese that detainees had to sleep standing up.[147]

Deportation from Ranong

Women and girls from brothels in the Ranong area who are arrested as illegal immigrants but not brought to the IDC in Bangkok have no choice about where they are to be deported -- they go straight into the arms of SLORC officials in Kawthaung. According to one report

---

[147] "Many Illegal Burmese Living in Tak Province," *Bangkok Post*, July 7, 1993.

we received, Thai police raided brothels in Ranong on July 16 and 25, 1992, arresting twenty Burmese women on the first occasion and seventeen on the second. All were sent directly to Kawthaung on the afternoon of July 25. They were arrested on return for leaving Burma illegally.[148]

> ● "Ma Thadar" was arrested in June 1992 with thirty other women in the Let Ywe Sin brothel in Ranong who, like her, were unable to run away fast enough. They were detained at the local immigration jail for eight days before being deported to Kawthaung by boat. As the boat approached the Kawthaung light house, the brothel owner and gun men stopped the boat. They gave money to the boatman, threatened the women at gunpoint onto their boat and returned them to the brothel.[149]

In the July 14, 1993 raids in Ranong in which 148 Burmese girls and women were arrested, fifty-eight were reportedly returned to SLORC officials in Kawthaung. According to reliable sources in Kawthaung, the women were sentenced to three years in prison for illegally leaving Burma. The remaining ninety women and girls are believed to be back in brothels in Ranong after the owners negotiated their fines with the local Thai authorities.

> ● "Myo Myo", whom we interviewed, believed that if she were arrested at the Old Victoria brothel in Ranong, she would be sent to the local police station and then deported to the Burmese authorities in Kawthaung. If the women and girls are pretty or popular at the brothel, she said, the owner's pimps will buy them back at the boat landing in Kawthaung form the Burmese

---

[148] Violation of the law banning illegal departure normally carries a six-month penalty (we have not been able to obtain the text of the law), but in this case, Thai NGOs reported that the women were reportedly sentenced to three years, with two additional years for having engaged in prostitution.

[149] Interview of the Burmese Students' Committee for Social Affairs, August 16, 1992.

authorities. She has seen many of the other girls returned this way.

Deportation From Kanchanaburi

As noted above, however, most IDC detainees prefer to be deported through Kanchanaburi Province. On average, one hundred detainees from the IDC are deported through Kanchanaburi every week, according to observers. The Thai-Burmese border there is controlled only in some sections on the Burmese side by SLORC, with minority militias, which are generally helpful to the deportees, controlling large stretches. There are also numerous refugee camps on the Thai side of the border for ethnic minorities fleeing military offensives in Burma. The refugees are also generally sympathetic to the deportees.

Nevertheless, deportation from Kanchanaburi is marked by such chaos, extortion and fear that women are often tempted to succumb to pressure to take offers for work in Thailand, even knowing that such jobs most likely will return them to the brothels, rather than proceed into Burma. The process works as follows:

Deportees are loaded onto buses in Bangkok for the three-and-a-half hour trip to the police lock-up in Kanchanaburi. They are held there for an average of seven days. This is the only province where deportees are routinely detained at the local immigration jail. The Kanchanaburi immigration jail is known among the Burmese to be one of the most abusive and corrupt jail along the border. Still the Burmese choose to pass through it if it allows them to avoid being directly handed over to SLORC upon deportation.

> ● On January 20, 1993, for example, "Muyar" and "Maw Maw" were transferred with over one hundred other detainees from IDC to Kanchanaburi. As they were waiting to get on the bus, a policeman began to grab and hug "Maw Maw" in the hallway in front of everyone. On the bus, all the women were told to sit by a windows to "guard them" from other inmates trying to escape. A policeman then told the inmates sitting besides "Maw Maw" to move and he sat next to her the whole way, touching her everywhere, kissing her and undressing her. Whenever "Maw Maw" tried to resist, he got very rough

with her. Everyone saw him but did not know what to do; the women in particular were afraid that they would be next.

Once in Kanchanaburi, the extortion and abuse continue. In the detention center in Kanchanaburi, girls and women reported paying extra to be put into a cell together with male inmates for safety against harassment from Thai police and immigration officers. Many of the women say they are married to one of the male deportees as a way of protecting themselves against abuse by the police. This stratagem, however, opens up possibilities for additional abuse.

The case of "Muyar" and "Maw Maw" is illustrative.

● On their first day in the Kanchanaburi jail, all of the women inmates from the IDC were asked to pay 100 baht ($4). If they said they had no money, the police "checked them out" touching all over their bodies. If they found any money, watches or other valuables, they took them. At night, the police charged women who claimed they were married 50 baht ($2) to sleep with their "husbands." If they did not or could not pay, the police said it was proof that they really were not married. Women often did not want to use their remaining funds to pay the fee, even if they were married, but everyone tried to pay to be "safe." Those not married would pick out another inmate and say it was their husband or allow another inmate to pay the 50 baht ($2) and take them as their wives. "Muyar" had her brother assume the role of her husband, but "Maw Maw" had some inmate she did not know pay for her.

One night, a policeman came to the women's cell and asked for "Maw Maw." "Muyar" felt very sorry for "Maw Maw" and knew she could not speak Thai, so she told the policeman that "Maw Maw" was very sick and could not get up. The policeman told "Muyar" to come down instead. "Muyar" refused. The policeman then entered the cell, pulled her out and beat her until she agreed to come down. When she got downstairs, the other policemen waiting asked their colleague, "Why didn't you get the pretty one?" "Muyar" told them "Maw Maw" was pregnant. Then the policemen asked "Muyar" why she was afraid to come down. "Muyar" said she had heard about how bad the Kanchanaburi policemen were.

When we interviewed "Muyar" at the deportation site on the border, she gave us a letter to bring back to others at the IDC, warning them not to return to Burma through Kanchanburi and telling them the rumors about the treatment of women there were true.

- "Soe Soe" was sent to Bangna police station and eventually transferred to the IDC. She was there for five days and then, on January 15, 1993, she was transferred with 170 other inmates to Kanchanaburi. Knowing the stories about Kanchanaburi, "Soe Soe" intentionally did not take a shower for weeks so she would look very ugly and dirty and no one would be interested in her. When she arrived at the jail, the police said the women could pay 100 baht ($4) to go upstairs with their husbands. Many inmates offered to pay for "Soe Soe," and she accepted a polite Burmese man who she thought was a student dissident. "Soe Soe" said she needed to have a husband for protection from the Thai police.

- "Aung Zeya," a Burmese male deported through Kanchanaburi, told us that on July 21, 1993 between three to four hundred detainees in the IDC were transferred to the Kanchanaburi immigration jail. There were approximately fifty women and fourteen children in the group. When they first arrived at the Kanchanaburi jail, they were divided by sex and put into small rooms downstairs. The women were asked to pay 100 baht ($4) for their transportation costs to the border and 100 baht ($4) for the cell upstairs. Ten women, including two girls aged fifteen, could not pay. One policeman and one male warden called them out and ordered them to take off all their clothes in front of all the other detainees. When several of the women were too slow, the two men pulled off their clothes. The policemen touched the women all over and even checked their vaginas. The police took everything they found on the women: watches, gold and money. Two officers played with the younger girls and after the search, sent everyone back to the cell except one girl, about 20 years old. Then the policemen asked the men were called forward. Those who could not pay were ordered to strip to their underwear while the two officers checked their clothes and watched as "room leaders" searched their underwear. All gold, money and valuable watches were confiscated. When this was completed all the deportees, except the one girl not returned to the group, were sent upstairs and placed into one of two cells, with no separation of male and female inmates. At 7 P.M. that night all the inmates upstairs could hear the police demanding that the girl left behind sleep with them. She refused, and they listened to at least an hour of screaming and beating. Afterwards, the same two officers brought her upstairs to the cell, slapping and hitting her in front of the others.

During the following eight days while this group was kept at the Kanchanaburi jail, the policemen came each night to the cell to call a woman or girl down to wash dishes. Those who refused to go down would be threatened and hit. Eventually all had to go.

One evening "Aung Zeya" heard the policemen tell the woman downstairs that if she agreed to sleep with him, she could return to Bangkok for free, without having to pay the 3,000 baht ($120) fee to return to the capital.

On the day of deportation, all deportees are loaded onto cargo trucks to standing capacity, locked in, driven to a place along the border and told to get out. Often the deportation point is out in a jungle (or given the extensive logging operations that have taken place here, the deforested vestige of what was once a jungle), far from any village or main roads. Many of the deportees find it difficult to walk after months in overcrowded jails, with little food and no exposure to the sun. Most have no food or water with them and have no idea where they are, what to do or how to survive.

Women face additional problems when they reach the deportation point, including abductions and solicitations from agents. There are often numerous agents who follow the trucks from nearby towns or know in advance the day and place of the deportation. They immediately approach the deportees offering jobs, transportation or other arrangements. In many cases, police officers themselves offer (for a price) to take the deportees back into Thailand. Since deportees rarely have this money, they are dependent on an agent willing to advance them the fee. This typically becomes the debt which the new recruit must work to repay. Many of the agents, while promising other forms of work, simply bring the women back to brothels to work off the new loan.

> ● "Maw Maw", for example, was deported from the Kanchanaburi jail on January 27, 1993 after having stayed there one week. Approximately 120 deportees were loaded onto a cargo truck and locked in. The police sat in front and never stopped for the three-hour drive. The deportees were taken to Panang Htaw, an abandoned refugee camp outside of Sangklaburi (in Kanchanaburi province). The police pointed out the direction to the border, and ordered the deportees to begin walking. They were escorted by armed Thai uniformed soldiers.[150] "Maw Maw" said ten other females had been deported with her. Seven of them went off with people offering jobs around the deportation site the first day. "Maw Maw" did not know what jobs they had been promised.

> ● "Soe Soe" told us of the Thai border patrol police abducting two young girls after they were deported and had found accommodation in the refugee camp for the night. She herself was deported from the Kanchanaburi jail on January 22, 1993 with about 170 other inmates. They were loaded onto two ten-wheel trucks like cattle

---

[150] The uniforms of the soldiers were described as light blue as worn by the Border Police Patrol units.

and locked in. It was so tight they all had to stand. Many people got sick. Several policemen sat up front. The trucks stopped in a field about an hour's walk from a camp for ethnic Mon refugees, and the detainees were told to get out. No one knew where to go, and some were so weak they could barely walk. They started walking towards the refugee camp. There were many border police checkpoints along the way, and many people around offering them transportation and jobs. "Soe Soe" and about twenty other deportees agreed to pay 160 baht ($6.20) for transport to the camp. When they arrived, they all were given shelter by refugees in the camp.

"Soe Soe" told us that on her first night at the camp two border police came on a motorcycle to the area where she was staying. It was about 8 P.M. and too dark to see the faces or uniforms of the police, but all the Mon refugees knew who they were by their motorcycle. The two police went from house to house asking for two young Chinese girls, aged fifteen and twenty-three, who had been deported that day. When they finally found them they took them to their base camp and returned them to the refugee camp later the next morning. The two Chinese would not talk to anyone and just hid. On the second night, the same members of the border patrol on the motorcycle took five other girls. Two returned the next morning. "Soe Soe" saw the three others down at the river with the border police on the morning that we interviewed her.

If the deportees withstand the initial onslaught of brokers and begin walking away, they soon realize over the next few days that they have little choice but to find some arrangement for work or at least transport back into Thailand. Most deportees could not begin to find their way back into Burma on their own, due to the war along the border and often their own disorientation. Some seek help from refugees or minority militia at the border to get home, but only in rare situations are they able to arrange a safe route back. Five days after a deportation, it is almost impossible to find any deportee left in the area.

Discreet Returns over the Border

For those not deported through standard deportation procedures, or who were not among the ninety-five women and girls officially repatriated in coordination with the Burmese authorities, discreet returns over the border are possible. The emergency shelters arrange discreet returns for the few Burmese girls and women they have taken in. These returns often involve a small group of girls and women brought to the border and given some transportation money to get home. Although the NGOs have tried to find ways to follow-up on those returned, in the majority of cases all contact is lost once they cross over the border.

In October 1992, the Thai and Burmese authorities opened up the road inside Burma from Taichelek to Keng Tung for tourists to travel inside this area for up to three days. This has given the NGOs an opportunity to try to visit some of the Burmese girls from villages along that route. However, visitors realize that contacts with foreigners do not go unnoticed in Burma, and it may not be entirely safe for the girls and women recently returned to meet and talk openly. However, the NGOs point out the value of having seen some of the girls back in their villages and knowing they made it home.

There have been instances where relatives working with NGOs to rescue family members have returned months later claiming their daughters, who had been discreetly returned, had never reached home. Due to the insecurity of the deportation procedures and failure of the state to organize them in a manner consistent with international law, deportation is unsafe, from the standpoint of basic physical security of the deportees. Male deportees who have not fled back into Thailand are known to have been arrested and forced to work as porters, carrying supplies for the Burmese army during its campaigns. It is not known whether any of the women deported from the Thai brothels suffered the same fate, although reports of women working as porters are numerous.

Deportation is rendered that much more problematic by the fact that once deported, the women and girls are in no legal position to pursue charges in Thailand against any parties implicated in their trafficking, forcible prostitution or other abuses against them.[151]

Summary Deportation: The Burmese Side

Women and girls deported across the border face the possibility of either being caught up in the border conflict if they attempt to find their way home or of being arrested by SLORC. According to Burmese Immigration and Manpower Act,[152] all Burmese illegally leaving the country are subject to arrest, fines and/or detention. The law is in direct violation of the Universal Declaration of Human Rights which states, in Article 13, that everyone has the right to leave and return to his or her own country.

Deportees handed over to Burmese authorities upon arrival in Burma are routinely arrested on charges of illegal departure. For example, in 1991, thirty people were taken in trucks to the center of Kawthaung town. When they arrived they were told by Burmese immigration police that they would be released only if they could pay 1,500 kyat ($250 by the official rate, $15 by the black market rate). If they could not pay the fine, they were told they would have to serve six months hard labor for "illegal departure."[153] Rarely can a Burmese

---

[151] Section 237 bis of Thailand's Criminal Procedure Code, as amended, does provide for the taking of testimony from witnesses to a crime in the cases where "there is reason to believe that a Witness who must be brought up for examination in the future shall be travelling out of the Kingdom...." Testimony taken from a witness in such a manner is admissible against a defendant in a criminal proceeding at a later date, when the Witness can no longer be summoned for examination, provided that the "alleged offender may cross examine or appoint a defense attorney to cross examine that witness." Unfortunately, the Burmese women and girls are rarely given an opportunity to charge their abusers as provided for by law, much less to have testimony taken from them prior to their deportation. It is impossible to pursue charges against an abuser once the women or girls has already left the country.

[152] An official Radio Rangoon report of July 3, 1991 corroborates these reports of fines of 1,500 kyat or six month prison terms under the Immigration and Manpower Act of the Union of Myanmar.

[153] Amnesty International, "*Thailand - Concerns about Treatment of Burmese Refugees*," ASA 39/15/91 (London: Amnesty International, August 1991).

afford the fine, and most are imprisoned unless a benefactor or agent can pay on their behalf. There are no exceptions for women and children.

Prostitution is illegal in Burma[154] so Burmese girls or women deported to Burma and suspected of having been a prostitute can face additional charges for prostitution and lengthy sentences. There is no evidence that the provisions of the Myanmar Penal Code and Code of Criminal Procedure, both of which guarantee "all persons detained...a just and fair trial by a competent court" are in fact respected.[155]   At the border, Burmese authorities have not shown any sensitivity to the issues of trafficking or to the victims. Only in the deportation of ninety-five women and girls from Pakkret on September 15, 1992 did SLORC offer an alternative to the typical cross-border deportation for the Burmese girls and women trafficked into brothels in Thailand and their near certain arrest or return.

No procedures are in place for monitoring or following up on deported Burmese.   SLORC authorities do not allow access, by international organizations or diplomats, to their border areas without SLORC escorts. No confidential interviews with individuals are allowed, and neither the United Nations High Commissioner for Refugees nor the International Committee of the Red Cross have access to detainees or deportees. The Special Rapporteur on Myanmar appointed by the U.N. Commission on Human Rights has met with a few selected political prisoners under highly controlled conditions.

However, consistent reports come back to Thailand of people, including deportees, being routinely arrested, detained, subjected to abuse and forced to porter for the military. Torture, rape and execution have been well documented by the United Nations bodies, international human

---

[154] There is a maximum three years sentence for prostituting or pimping in Burma. Reported in *Myanmar Children in Especially Difficult Circumstances*, Dr. Jocelyn Boyden, UNICEF consultant, February 1992.

[155] According to Professor Yozo Yokota, United Nations Special Rapporteur on Myanmar, "Only in cases for 'minor' crimes for which punishment would not exceed one year, may [suspects] in certain circumstances be tried in a summary manner." *Report to the Commission on Human Rights*, February 17, 1993, p.37.

rights organizations and governments.[156]

The women and girls may also be caught up in counterinsurgency operations by the Burmese military. Offensives conducted by the military against the ethnic insurgencies along the Thai-Burmese border have resulted in systematic abuses against civilians; the women may fall victim to such abuses as they try to traverse contested areas to get back to their villages. Often the Burmese military recruits porters from the jails, and women and children are no exception.

In addition, the military offensives often result in incursions into Thai territory in hot pursuit of armed rebels, or abduction of Thai nationals, or in some cases, actual military clashes between Thai and Burmese armed forces. These incidents usually occur during the annual dry season offensives of the Burmese army against ethnic insurgents, from late November to early February. In early 1992, in an offensive against the Karen ethnic rebels, Burmese forces spilled over into Thailand, and Thai planes strafed the Burmese units in retaliation. A local Thai official of the Tak province chamber of commerce was detained by the Burmese army, and armed Burmese searched Thai boats along the Moei River.[157] A year later, in an incident in the same area, Burmese troops fired mortars from their side into a Thai village. They then crossed the border and set fire to huts, apparently believing the village was sheltering rebels.

When the Thai military arrests Burmese soldiers for crossing the border, the Burmese retaliate by arresting Thais, usually civilians who have come across for trade or timber. In March 1993, five Thai villagers were held for two weeks by the Burmese military until the Thai army released two soldiers it had captured. The Thai villagers were fined for

---

[156] Report on the Situation of Human Rights in Myanmar, prepared by Yozo Yokota, Special Rapporteur of the Commission on Human Rights, February 17, 1993, E/CN.4/1993/37. Also see: Amnesty International, Thailand-Concerns About Treatment of Burmese Refugees, ASA 39/15/91, August 1991, p.4.

[157] See, for example, "Burmese Fighting Spills Over into Southern Thailand," The Nation, January 23, 1992. To prevent such incidents from turning into major diplomatic crises and negotiate border crossings, a series of Thai-Burmese Border Committee meetings have been held since December 1988.

illegally entering Burma, and each had to pay about 1,800 baht ($72).[158] The dangers of Burmese women and girls deported and left to find their own way home along the border are thus formidable.

There is also the possibility that the women may be forced back into prostitution. The same Burmese officials who turned a blind eye to or actively colluded in the trafficking to Thailand may await the women on the other side.

G. THE NON-PENAL ALTERNATIVE: OFFICIAL REPATRIATION

For the most part, Burmese women were lured into Thailand and were forced to prostitute themselves in what amounted to a form of bonded labor. If, because of illegally leaving the country and working as prostitutes, they are then liable to arrest and persecution on the Burmese side of the border, they should be treated as trafficking victims and not summarily deported as illegal immigrants. Instead, in a manner consistent with their own anti-trafficking laws and international norms, the Thai government should provide the means to ensure that the women and girls are not punished, and the Burmese government should ensure that international agencies such as the ICRC, UNHCR, or relevant international NGOs, undertake frequent and systematic monitoring of the returnees safety and well-being.

The Thai government has, on occasion, recognized that no sound legal justification exists for arresting, detaining and summarily deporting the Burmese trafficking victims. During the Anand Administration, as noted in the background section above, the arrest and summary deportation of Burmese trafficking victims as prostitutes and/or illegal immigrants was briefly halted. The new approach, described in detail below, was riddled with problems. Nonetheless, it did lay the groundwork for more equitable treatment of the Burmese women and girls.

For a brief period in 1992, rather than arresting and imprisoning the girls as illegal immigrants, then Minister Saisuree arranged for at least one group of them, primarily composed of women arrested in the June and July 1992 raids, to be sent to the penal reform institution of Pakkret pending an officially sanctioned repatriation in cooperation with the Burmese authorities. From June through July 1992, the majority of

---

[158] "Burma Frees Five Thai Villagers", *The Nation*, March 3, 1993.

the Burmese women and girls "rescued" from brothels were sent to Pakkret.

On July 30, 1992, the Deputy Foreign Minister, U Nyunt Swe, met with Minister Saisuree to discuss the return of the nearly 150 Burmese recently rescued from brothels in Thailand.[159] Burma however, would only agree to the return of its nationals of "Burman stock" as opposed to hilltribes or members of any of Burma's ethnic minorities.[160] When Burmese embassy officials went to Pakkret, only Burman women were brought forward to meet them. Hilltribe girls and women from Burma who could not speak Burmese were not introduced.

Following the embassy visit, ninety-five of the approximate 150 women and girls were considered Burmese nationals and therefore eligible for the official repatriation. On September 15, 1992, the ninety-five women officially repatriated to Burma. Three were under eighteen years old. The rest were between eighteen and thirty-six years old. Forty-three of the women were HIV positive. Two hilltribe women from the Aka ethnic group who were added to the ninety-five from Pakkret, as described below, were separated from the other women in the Burmese town of Keng Tung and turned over to local authorities.

When the ninety-five were deported they were accompanied by Burmese officials to Taichelek, Burma.[161] There was no international monitoring in place for these returnees once in Burma and little information has been available as to what happened subsequent to their return. U Nyunt Swe dismissed widespread fears of what would happen

---

[159]"Ambassador Seeks Return Home of Burmese Women", *Bangkok Post,* July 31, 1992.

[160] "Burman" refers to ethnicity, "Burmese" to nationality. The SLORC government in Burma has engaged in its own version of ethnic cleansing. Official discrimination against non-Burmans goes back to the citizenship law of 1982, which gave full citizenship only to Burmese who could trace the families of both parents back to pre-1824 Burma. Some ten percent of the population who could not meet this criterion were considered non-nationals and classified as "associate" or "naturalized" citizens. The purpose was to deny full citizenship to ethnic minority groups. SLORC has also engaged in systematic persecution of non-Burman ethnic groups, including the Muslim Rohingya, over 300,000 of whom have fled to Bangladesh.

[161] "Sex Slaves Sent Home," *Bangkok Post,* September 16, 1992.

to the women:

> We will take back anyone who is a true Burmese
> citizen...We have no policy to mistreat our own people.
> Those repatriated to Burma will be screened by
> photographic identification to establish that they are
> genuine citizens before receiving medical check-ups and
> necessary treatment...[162]

U Ye Myint, a Burmese Embassy spokesman, later claimed forty-three of the returnees remained in Rangoon for medical treatment as they were found to be HIV positive, while fifty-two were rest were sent back to their home towns and villages, mainly in the southern Mon State.[163] On November 19, U Nyunt Swe invited Dr. Saisuree to meet with a group of the ninety-five women she helped repatriate, but as of July 1993, neither she nor any other Thai official had been to Burma to do so.[164]

This official repatriation process was plagued by problems. The Thai government's willingness to return only ethnic Burman women and girls made it complicit in the ethnic discrimination practiced by SLORC. Dr. Saisuree claimed the Thai government was considering alternative measures for the remaining Burmese girls and women from ethnic minority groups, but to our knowledge, no such measures were undertaken.[165]

No legal justification whatsoever exists for detaining the women and girls in a penal reform institution prior to deportation. The choice of Pakkret to hold the women and girls was in fact punitive and amounted to arbitrary detention -- often for longer than six months -- without charge or trial.

---

[162] "Thai-Burmese Plan to Stem Flow of Illegal Workers," *The Nation*, September 16, 1993.

[163] "Saisuree Invited to Rangoon," *The Nation*, November 20, 1992.

[164] Ibid.

[165] "Saisuree Defends Plan to Repatriate Burmese Women," *The Nation*, August, 20, 1992.

If the alternative to summary deportation of the women and girls is to proceed fairly and effectively, non-penal shelters must be located for the girls pending their repatriation. Dr. Saisuree recognized this fact when we interviewed her on March 4, 1993. She told us

> although the initiative was first introduced through the Pakkret system, I hope to work closely with the NGOs as an alternative to Pakkret.[166]

Moreover, although Saisuree repeatedly pledged to monitor the safety of the women and girls after their return to Burma, no official effort has been made to do so. The fate of the returned women and girls, and thus the viability of the official repatriation process, has yet to be fully determined.

Despite the serious problems with the initiative, this official repatriation appears to have enabled many of the women to return to their parents safely.

"Nyunt Nyunt" was thirty-five years old and was among the ninety-five officially deported back to Burma. She later returned to Thailand to find her husband, and we interviewed her there.

> ● "Nyunt Nyunt" was "rescued" from a brothel in Ranong on July 7, 1992 and sent to Pakkret the following day. She stayed there until the repatriation began on September 15. She said they arrived in Taichelek at 10:00 A.M. on September 16 and were sent to the Than Lwin Oo Hotel. In the hotel they had their blood tested and were given injections and medicine tablets. The Burmese immigration officers questioned the girls and women about who had brought them to Thailand and how long they had been there.
>
> At 6 P.M. on the following day, the women and girls were loaded onto military cargo trucks and sent to Keng Tung. They were very frightened because they had heard rumors of what happened to Burmese prostitutes -- such as arrest and even execution if found HIV positive -- when they returned to Burma. On September 17 at

---

[166] Interview with Dr. Saisuree Chutikul, March 4, 1993.

5:00 A.M. they arrived in Keng Tung. There they were threatened by the Burmese authorities, who warned them that this was the last time they would be given "special treatment." In Keng Tung, the two Aka girls were handed over to the local office of the Law and Order Restoration Council. The remaining ninety-five were sent to the Chin Rifle Number 4 compound and stayed there from September 17 to 19.

On September 19, according to "Nyunt Nyunt", they were sent from Keng Tung to Rangoon by plane. They were taken directly to the North Okkalapa Female Police Training Academy in Rangoon. One planeload was given one room and the other planeload another room. They had to take tablets and get injections every day. Everyone learned who had tested HIV+ for the AIDS virus, including thirty-two women and one baby. All thirty-two received a special lecture from a Dr. Myat Kyaw. He told them they had to come back to the academy every month and gave them a medical document.

The women were told that they could go home as soon as their parents came to collect them. Family members had to show their identification and to document their relationship to the women. Girls and women were released to their parents beginning in the middle of October, or about a month after the deportation took place. "Nyunt Nyunt" was released on October 30; when she left, half of the women were still waiting for their parents. Some girls came from far away from Rangoon and from very poor families, and it was not clear if their families would be able to come.

"Nyunt Nyunt" believes that if certain safeguards are in place, such as the availability of non-penal shelters, a non-discriminatory approach to potential returnees and adequate follow-up to ensure the safety of returnees, such official deportations are the only way for the women and girls to return to Burma. Too many others have an interest in their remaining in Thailand or on the border -- their old owners and agents, new traffickers, the police, border police and immigration officers, both

Thai and Burmese. Without an official escort, they would only be able to return home if they had sufficient money to pay the necessary bribes, and none of them do.

Unfortunately, rather than further refining this approach and establishing non-penal shelters and official repatriation procedures for trafficking victims (barring any well-founded fear of persecution on return to Burma), the Chuan administration appears to have abandoned it entirely. In an interview with us on March 4, Colonel Surasak, chief of the Crime Suppression Division, told us that all of the Burmese women and girls arrested in the crackdowns would be sent to the Immigration Detention Center (IDC) and deported.

VI. NON-GOVERNMENTAL ORGANIZATIONS (NGOs)

Given the failure of the Thai government to suppress the trafficking in women by enforcing its own laws, some observers have proposed that non-governmental organizations (NGOs), particularly local Thai groups, might be able to take on a larger role in addressing the problem. But NGOs should not be expected to make up for shortcomings of the government, nor would provision of extra resources to these overstretched organizations do more than increase a demand for services which government failures are fuelling.

NGOS IN THAILAND

NGOs, both Thai and international, working on trafficking-related problems, vary widely in their programs and objectives. Their work includes tracing networks to assist families in finding their daughters; monitoring the extent of trafficking, conditions in the brothels, and other abuses; negotiating for the release of women wrongfully arrested and providing temporary shelter and training when possible; advocacy and legal counselling; public awareness initiatives; and a forum for policy discussions and recommendations.

Given the fact that Thailand has one of the strongest NGO movements in Asia, with several hundred organizations playing an active and critical role in addressing social issues, there are surprisingly few working on women's and children's rights specifically. We are aware of approximately thirty NGOs which focus on a wide spectrum of women and children's concerns. Of these, less than ten have addressed in any way the Burmese girls and women described in this report. Most are based in Bangkok, with others located in Chiangmai, Chiangrai and along the Thai-Burmese border. The majority of these NGOs are Thai, although a few are operated by Burmese exiles in Thailand; we are aware of only two international NGOs with programs specifically designed to reach Burmese girls and women trafficked into brothels in Thailand.

Although the local NGOs have established contact with various government agencies and in some cases work with the Crime Suppression Division to follow up on specific cases of trafficked women and girls, they generally have not been consulted on government strategies or policy decisions. At the same time, the Thai government has called upon the expertise of some NGOs, including the Burmese groups, for interpreting, investigation, "rescues" and arranging returns of Burmese to their country.

All NGOs working on women's and children's rights in Thailand are quickly overwhelmed by the magnitude and complexity of the trafficking problem, the extent of the abuses and needs, the sensitivity with which they must be addressed -- and their own limited resources. To work on trafficking is to be drawn into a wide array of concerns including the trafficking of rural or hilltribe women and children within Thailand; the trafficking of Thai women and children internationally to places such as Japan; the importing of "illegals" from abroad to work in Thailand or transit through Thailand to other international markets; the growth in of sex tourism in Thailand and inherent abuses; health concerns and the impact of the sweeping AIDS virus; and the involvement of government officials and criminals at all levels.

The trafficking in Burmese girls and women is a particularly sensitive issue as the Thai government has not articulated a clear or consistent policy towards Burma, Burmese asylum seekers or illegal immigrants. There are frequent government warnings of arrest and fines for anyone known to house or support an illegal Burmese in Thailand. At the same time, there is no single Thai policy on trafficking or on treatment of victims. The policy differs from agency to agency and from one administration to another. NGOs thus have little option other than to negotiate quietly with individual officials who are frequently changing. As a result, most of the NGOs working most directly with us did not want their names or those of their organization disclosed for fear that their ability to operate confidentially and cooperate with government offices and officials would be undermined.

One Thai NGO involved in many of the issues addressed in this report is a case in point. It has taken a high-profile role in speaking to the abuses and intervening on behalf of Burmese girls and women trafficked into Thai brothels. Its mandate is to trace, rescue, provide legal advice and offer temporary shelter as necessary to children whose rights are being violated. At the same time, it works to promote respect for the rights of children and young women in law and government policy. It has worked closely with the Crime Suppression Division (CSD) of the Thai police force and Thai government officials to rescue and shelter children and young adults physically or sexually abused, abandoned or forced into bonded labor or prostitution.

Initially, this NGO focused primarily on Thai nationals. In 1990, however it began reaching out to children trafficked into Thailand from neighboring countries. In 1992 alone, it had assisted 452 children working under conditions of slavery or young adults in life-threatening situations. Over half of its caseload were girls or young women rescued from brothels, of which more than one third were from Burma.[167]

Working with children and young adults from neighboring countries has added additional problems for clients and staff, such as illegal immigration status, possibility of detention and deportation, language and cultural barriers, and fear of human rights abuses in their country of origin.

When the NGO provides temporary shelter to women and children, it takes on the added responsibility of finding safe, unpublicized ways to get them home over the border. In addition, an overwhelming percentage of those brought to the shelter are found to be HIV positive. For example, in a rescue this NGO carried out in cooperation with the CSD in 1991, nineteen girls were rescued (fifteen of them from Burma) and all but two tested HIV positive. The dilemma of how to inform the girls of the virus, testing, the results and future in the context of life in repressive Burma is a further responsibility. Finally, this particular NGO has a core staff of approximately 30 to cover the entire spectrum of its work.

In an effort to cope with the onslaught of issues, local Thai NGOs and international organizations have established working groups to share information, strategies, coordinate intervention and advocacy activities and provide a united voice to government policy and actions. The international network to End of Child Prostitution in Asian Tourism (ECPAT) was formed in 1990. In 1991, NGOs in Thailand formed a national committee entitled Thailand's End of Sexploitation of Children in Tourism (TESCT). The same year the Working Group to End Sexploitation in Thailand was established to address the wider issues of trafficking and need to prosecute the traffickers, brothel owners, pimps and others involved in protecting the racket. These consortiums of NGOs provide a collective platform for speaking out on such sensitive issues as trafficking and the role of the state. They also provide a protective cover

---

[167] This is according to the NGO's end of the year reports for 1990 - 1992.

for individual NGOs, sharing the risks and enabling them to turn to a larger body for support.

Together, the Thai NGOs have been pushing the Thai authorities to adopt the necessary domestic legislation and ratify the relevant international instruments to create a sound approach to trafficking in conformity with international norms. They have proposed several key changes in Thailand's Anti-Trafficking and Anti-Prostitution laws and have called on the government to ratify the Trafficking Convention and the International Covenant on Civil and Political Rights. As of January 1994, these efforts had yet to yield concrete results.

Although the Anand and Chuan administrations have spoken positively of the work of Thai NGOs, the NGOs themselves have felt increasing pressure by the government to keep a low profile.

But even if the NGOs working with Burmese women and children had no limits on their resources and no pressure from the government, there would still be serious constraints on the extent to which they, as NGOs, could intervene on behalf of the Burmese girls and women. Unlimited direct assistance to victims of trafficking will not address the root cause of the problem in the absence of effective action against the traffickers, recruiters, brothel owners and complicit government officials. For instance, when the possibility arose that private funds might be available to expand their shelters for children and young adults "rescued" from slavery conditions, NGOs explained that the demand for shelters would continue to increase was long as the trafficking and slavery issues go unaddressed.

Most of the NGOs we interviewed were adamant that their work as advocates for change through research, community outreach, legal counselling and international publicity was not intended to replace or substitute for government action, and the government had responsibilities that could not be undertaken directly by NGOs. They are not in a position to enforce the law or negotiate an agreement with the Burmese government for the safe return of those trafficked into Thailand. The NGOs, however, strongly believed that they could play a valuable consultative role to inform and encourage the efforts of the Thai government while ensuring the rights of women and children are upheld.

NGOS IN BURMA

In Burma, no indigenous NGOs are allowed to operate. At most, religious institutions attempt to discreetly offer services to assist poor communities, but even they are under considerable pressure to maintain a low profile and are often themselves victims of abuse by SLORC authorities. Very few independent international NGOs have been willing to work in Burma for fear of giving legitimacy to SLORC, even if they could obtain access. (A few NGOs, such as World Vision, are operating in Burma.) The absence of NGOs complicates the task of the United Nations Development Program (UNDP), the most important U.N. agency operating in Burma, which has come under criticism for continuing to channel funds through Burmese authorities to areas controlled by SLORC, rather than to border areas where humanitarian aid may be most critically needed. Partly in response to this criticism, UNDP sent a task force to Burma in late 1993 that recommended that its programs in Burma be carried out by NGOs under UNDP supervision. These programs include HIV education and prevention strategies.

VII. CAPTIVE PARTNERS: FORCED PROSTITUTION AND HIV/AIDS

For the majority of Burmese women and girls trafficked into Thailand for the purposes of forced prostitution, the human rights abuses they experience will ultimately prove fatal. Of the nineteen Burmese women and girls we interviewed who had been tested for HIV, fourteen were found to be infected with the virus, which causes the deadly acquired immunodeficiency syndrome (AIDS).[168] This rate of infection is roughly three times higher than among prostitutes more generally in Thailand.[169] In our view, the high rate is directly attributable to the Thai government's failure to protect the Burmese women and girls against trafficking, forced labor, and other abuses and to investigate and prosecute the abusers, including Thai officials.

This section documents how sexual enslavement of Burmese women and girls, through debt bondage, physical coercion and psychological intimidation, leads to their HIV infection. Brothel owners and their accomplices who compel Burmese women and girls to have involuntary and often unprotected sex with numerous partners every day are in effect enforcing a dangerous game of sexual Russian roulette: it is only a matter of time before the women and girls contract HIV.

We also examine the range of abuses suffered by women and girls on account of their suspected or actual HIV infection, abuses often perpetrated in the name of AIDS prevention and control. Burmese women and girls are tested by brothel owners and by public health officials for HIV without their informed consent, sometimes without even their knowledge. Those who are aware of the purpose of the HIV test are often denied the results of their own tests, even as the outcomes are made available to brothel owners, immigration officials and others. The breach of confidentiality not only violates the right of the Burmese women and girls to privacy but may have dangerous consequences for

---

[168] HIV inevitably develops into AIDS, which weakens the body's natural immune systems and leaves it vulnerable to opportunistic diseases, eventually causing death. There is no known cure for AIDS at the present time.

[169] In 1991, HIV infection trends among female prostitutes in Thailand was said to be 21.6 percent according to the World Health Organization (WHO) in "AIDS/HIV infection in South-East Asia," November 7, 1992.

their treatment at the hands of the SLORC after deportation.

A. ABUSES THAT LEAD TO HIV INFECTION

        Awareness of AIDS among potential customers has driven the Thai sex industry to supply more and more young girls from remote villages that are perceived to be untouched by AIDS. Brothel owners employ various means of control already discussed -- debt bondage, illegal confinement, use or threat of physical force, and psychological intimidation -- to keep the Burmese women and girls in sexual slavery until their debts are repaid. The Burmese are powerless to negotiate any terms of sex, such as condom use, that might protect them from HIV infection, just as they have virtually no choice of customer, no say over how many customers to accept in a given day or the type of sex in which they will engage.

        Young girls, sometimes only thirteen or fourteen years old, may be particularly at risk. Not only are they often too intimidated even to attempt to negotiate the terms of sex, but preliminary medical research suggests that the younger the girl, the more susceptible she may be to HIV infection for physiological reasons.[170] (The average age of the trafficking victims we interviewed was seventeen.)

        Burmese women and girls who attempt to refuse customers often face retaliation. Sometimes, the owners and pimps threaten them with physical harm, or allow the customers to do so.

> ● "Tar Tar" had been moved around to different brothels since she was sixteen years old. In some of them, condoms were available, but it was up to the men if they used them or not. Most did not. At one brothel, Dao Kanong, the owner did not supply condoms, so she bought them herself. If the client refused, she tried to argue, but the owner forced her. Once, he threatened

---

[170] Because the mucous membrane of the genital tract in girls is not as thick as that of a grown women, medical researchers have hypothesized that it is a less efficient barrier to viruses. Moreover, young women may be less efficient than older women in producing mucous, which has an immune function. United Nations Development Program, "Young Women: Silence, Susceptibility and the HIV Epidemic."

her with a gun and told her not to leave the room again. Many of her customers were uniformed police and soldiers.

- "Kyi Kyi" worked every day and had at least four to five clients a day. If she did not agree to a client or his demands she was beaten by the owner. She tried to escape in 1991, but the owner caught her and took her to the kitchen and beat her with a very thick wooden stick. The owner told her if she tried to escape again, he would shoot her with a gun. He then took a pistol out and put it to her head and said, "Like this."

- Five days after arriving at the brothel, "Myo Myo" had to take Thai clients. At that time, she tried to escape. The client slapped her and held her back. She finally ran out of the room. Two pimps and the owner caught and beat her. Thu Za [wife of the brothel owner] told her to be quiet and try to do what she was told so she would not get killed.

Other times, owners simply remind the girls that they are trapped until they work off their debt.

- When "Tin Tin" was first brought to the Sanae brothel in Klong Yai, she was told to go into a windowed room and given a number. Then she realized it was prostitution and she did not want to do it. For a month, she tried to refuse. During this time she saw others slapped in the face and hit hard. She knew she had no choice. The owner and pimps were always saying, "If you want to go home then you've got to work or you'll never pay back your debt." Then she was given a client and sold as a virgin. That month she had four clients all paying for her virginity. She was always kept in a special room for the virgin period. She never dared to say no to a client or leave him once in the room. She saw other girls come out before a client and the pimps beat them. She did not want to agree to anything. It was all forced.

After the initial period when the girls are sold as virgins to just a few men, the number of customers multiplies, sometimes to as many as ten to fifteen a day, any of whom could be a source of infection. As a result, a majority of Burmese girls who start out as young, "clean" virgins become infected after working in the closed brothels after about six months.[171]

What emerges from our interviews is a pattern of transmission from male customers to young girls that shatters the common perception that prostitutes are the "source" of HIV/AIDS. To be sure, once infected, the Burmese girls in the brothels are likely to infect their customers. But whereas their clients can choose to use condoms and to abstain from sex, the women and girls have no such choice; they are captive partners.

B. THAI GOVERNMENT ACCOUNTABILITY

The Thai government is well aware of both the plight of Burmese women and girls trapped in forced prostitution and the danger posed by the AIDS pandemic. But it has consistently failed to investigate and prosecute police officers and other traffickers who are implicated in the illegal trade in women and girls. Moreover, the government's two-fold strategy for combatting AIDS -- law enforcement and health intervention -- for the most part targets Burmese women and girls as illegal immigrants and vectors of transmission, while largely exempting procurers, brothel owners, pimps and clients from punishment under the law. As indicated by the girls' extremely high rates of infection, the strategy has utterly failed to put an end to human rights abuses that result in the Burmese women and girls becoming HIV-infected.

The central government has long been aware of the existence of illegal brothels but has been slow to address the health risks to the women and girls in them. Until 1991, the Thai government resolutely ignored the problem. For example, in 1990 then Prime Minister Chatichai Choonhavan refused to chair a 1990 AIDS conference because he feared it would create panic. His administration also tried to prevent concerned groups, including NGOs, from addressing the spread of AIDS

---

[171] Interview with ACCESS, February 4, 1993, Bangkok. ACCESS is a Thai NGO dedicated to campaigns for AIDS prevention, understanding HIV/AIDS and forms of discrimination against those found with HIV/AIDS, and support services for those with HIV/AIDS and their families.

publicly.[172]   This was motivated in part by denial, since AIDS at first was perceived as a "foreigners' disease."

A more reprehensible reason for official inaction was a desire to protect the tourism industry, of which sex tourism is a major component, against a slowdown in demand stemming from fears about HIV/AIDS. The sex industry constitutes a wealthy and powerful lobby group whose interests cannot be easily ignored in the formulation of official policy regarding trafficking and prostitution.   Political pressures aside, by attracting visitors who bring in foreign exchange, sex tourism has been a significant source of income for the Thai government itself, not just the traffickers, brothel owners, and individual complicit officials.[173]

Beginning in 1989, the Ministry of Public Health adopted an aggressive policy of seeking to place "a box of one hundred condoms in every bedroom of every commercial sex establishment, especially low-fee sex establishments, at no charge."[174] But it was not until Chatichai was deposed by a military coup in February 1991, and an interim administration established under then Prime Minister Anand Panyarachun, that the government began a serious and aggressive AIDS prevention and education campaign. Anand took several important steps to control HIV/AIDS.   He created the AIDS Policy, Planning and Coordination Bureau within the Prime Minister's Permanent Secretary's Office to coordinate HIV/AIDS prevention. Anand also appointed Mechai Viravaidya, a leading proponent of AIDS education and condom use, to the National AIDS Committee. Finally, his administration formulated an inter-agency approach, with technical and human rights guidelines, to control the pandemic which is laid out in the "National AIDS Prevention

---

[172] Pyne, *AIDS and Prostitution in Thailand.* p.47

[173] It is difficult to know the exact percentage of visitors to Thailand who are there specifically for sex tourism.   However, two-thirds of the estimated five million tourists who visit Thailand each year are male, and twenty percent are single men who go to Thailand for day trips from Malyasia and Singapore. "Sex and Death in Thailand," *Newsweek*, July 20, 1992.

[174]AIDSCAP/Family Health International, USA, "The Use of Sexually Transmitted Disease (STD) Statistics to Evaluate Thailand's HIV Prevention Program," speech presented at 9th International Conference on AIDS, Berlin, Germany, June 10, 1993.

Plan for 1992-1996."[175] Anand Panyarachun was only the second head of state in the world to decide to chair a national AIDS committee.

Since the restoration of a democratically elected government in September 1992, the national HIV/AIDS program appears to be undergoing further change. Leadership of the program has reverted back to the Ministry of Public Health and budget allocations for AIDS prevention to other ministries have been scaled back, with still unclear results. The National AIDS Committee has not met since 1991.[176]

In any case, until the Burmese women and girls are freed from sexual bondage, the government's large-scale condom distribution campaigns are of no help to them. Condoms are irrelevant where no capacity to negotiate sex exists. For condoms to aid in the prevention of HIV transmission, they must be used during every act of intercourse. In addition, the women and girls have to be able to negotiate the number of customers accepted each day. Otherwise, the use of condoms could heighten the probability of HIV infection. When girls are forced to have sex with many customers each day, condom use often leads to friction sores which may facilitate viral transmission.[177]

---

[175] These guidelines were adopted by the Thai Cabinet on September 1, 1992 and are the basis for external scientific, technical or financial support granted under the auspices of WHO. According to WHO guidelines: "Existence of a medium-term (3-5 years) WHO-approved National AIDS Plan should be a prerequisite for the provision of external support except for urgently required support." Moreover, "all projects supported by external donors should be executed as an integral part of National AIDS Control Programs, respecting their Plan of Operations, and within the management structure established by the relevant governments; i.e. provided in a manner that... ensures the equal and non-discriminatory treatment of *all* HIV-infected persons" (emphasis in original). "Guiding objectives and principles for the comprehensive coordination of global and national AIDS activities," Fifth meeting of the Participating Parties, WHO Global Program on AIDS, Geneva, 27-28 April 1988.

[176] Vitit Muntabhorn, *HIV/AIDS, Ethics and the Law: The Case of Thailand*, May 1993 (draft).

[177] In particular, there appears to be an association between HIV infection and the incidence of cervical ectopy. Various studies have postulated that the cervix is the most likely site of HIV infection in women. United Nations Development Program, "Young Women: Silence, Susceptibility and the HIV

Moreover, the effect of attempting to address the health concerns of the women and girls unaccompanied by a vigorous campaign to free these women and girls who are held in the brothels through bondage, illegal confinement and threats or use of physical force, and to prosecute their abusers to the fullest extent of law, amounts to the state winking at sexual slavery.

The failure of the central government to enforce the law puts local health officials in a difficult position. If they refuse to enter the brothels, they may be knowingly contributing to the spread of a grave public health hazard and failing to provide medical care to those in need. If they enter in their official capacities and declare the women and girls either "clean" or "infected," they appear to be rubberstamping an illegal industry. Many of the health officials are motivated by good intentions and carefully avoid any actions that might further jeopardize the well-being of the girls. But the ethical dilemma is a stark one: if they remain silent so as to avoid antagonizing the brothel owner and maintaining access to the women and girls in the brothel, they are failing to publicize abuses in the brothels and the danger of AIDS in a way that might prevent more cases from developing.[178]

That provincial health officials have to make the onerous choice between providing health care and exposing human rights abuses is intolerable. The national Crime Suppression Division and local police

---

Epidemic." The newly-developed female condom is too expensive for most women in low-cost brothels, even assuming they can get their customer to agreed to its use. The Thai government is not distributing the female condom free of charge as it does the male condom.

[178] Interview with a Thai NGO, July 29, 1993. In one example of the ethical dilemma, a group of fourteen brothel owners in Mae Sai district of Chiangrai province in northern Thailand threatened in 1992 to deny health workers continued access to their brothels for research if the chief of the district public health division hurt their businesses by creating a public scare about AIDS. In response, the local police chief mediated a compromise allowing provincial health officials to continue to research AIDS in the brothels, but barring them from conducting AIDS awareness programs in the brothels or publicly. To date, the Mae Sai district hospital has not campaigned about the number of people who are HIV positive or who have died of AIDS in the district. Instead, they are quietly counselling and providing homecare for AIDS patients and their families.

should be vigorously enforcing the anti-trafficking and rape provisions on the books so that health personnel would not have to make ethical compromises. Absent genuine law enforcement, there is little incentive for health officials to report suspected abuses. They cannot expect the police to conduct impartial investigations, given the known extent of police involvement in protecting prostitution rings.

Given the reality that the brothels will not be easily nor quickly eradicated, we do not advocate that all attempts to address the health concerns of the women and girls, including HIV testing, should cease. However, the Thai Ministry of Public Health must take all necessary measures to ensure that no further testing is conducted without the voluntary informed consent of the Burmese women and girls, that their test results are treated in the strictest confidence by authorized health personnel, and that the patients are told their test outcomes upon request. As of January 1994, this was not the case.

C. ABUSES ARISING FROM PERCEIVED OR ACTUAL HIV STATUS

Notwithstanding greater openness in Thailand's official efforts to address the AIDS pandemic, the government's treatment of Burmese trafficking victims suspected or known to have HIV/AIDS has resulted in further violations of their basic human rights.

Mandatory HIV testing

HIV testing of Burmese women and girls in the sex industry is conducted not for the purpose of estimating general HIV prevalence levels,[179] but rather to identify individuals who may be HIV positive

---

[179] Random testing by public health personnel for the purpose of estimating HIV prevalence levels is acceptable under international legal standards regarding medical practices, provided that two conditions are met. The blood that is tested must be a small portion of a sample that was drawn, with the patient's consent, for some other purpose. And the sample must be kept strictly anonymous. The screening of Burmese women and girls in the brothels does not fall within this category of testing.   UN Center for Human Rights and World Health Organization (WHO), *Report of an International Consultation on AIDS and Human Rights*, Geneva, July 26-28, 1989, [UN:New York, 1991], p.56.

or who have AIDS. It is frequently imposed on a mandatory basis, without informed consent, on women and girls working in Thai brothels, in detention at Pakkret, and reportedly by SLORC after deportation. Mandatory testing without informed consent is explicitly prohibited by both World Health Organization (WHO) Guidelines[180] and the Thai National AIDS Plan.[181]

Mandatory testing for HIV has no basis in either international or Thai law. On the contrary, it constitutes an unjustifiable interference with the individual's basic right to privacy.[182] The right to privacy is not absolute under international law. Governments may derogate from that right in order to protect public health,[183] but only if three stringent conditions are met. There must be "a specific law which is

---

[180] The UN Human Rights Center and WHO jointly concluded that "mandatory testing of any individuals (other than voluntary donors of blood, semen, or other tissue or organs) for HIV infection, no matter how they are selected" would "constitute interference with the right to privacy of the individuals concerned, and would not be justifiable under international human rights law on public health (or any other) grounds." UN Human Rights Center and WHO, *AIDS and Human Rights*, p. 55.

[181] According to Thailand National AIDS Prevention Plan, "[t]here should be no compulsory testing for AIDS *without* exception unless the person or his/her legal representative gives fully informed consent..." (emphasis added), p. 23.

[182] Universal Declaration of Human Rights, Art. 12 states "No one shall be subjected to arbitrary interference with his [sic] privacy ... Everyone has the right to the protection of the law against such interference ..."

[183] While the Universal Declaration on Human Rights does not delimit the right to privacy, subsequent regional treaties expound on the grounds for derogation. The European Convention for the Protection of Human Rights and Fundamental Freedoms is most specific regarding what are acceptable grounds for derogating the right to privacy. Article 8 of the European Convention explicitly lists "the protection of health or morals" as one of these grounds. The American Convention on Human Rights, by prohibiting "arbitrary or abusive interference," leaves room for interference that arguably serves the public good. The African Charter on Human and Peoples' Rights does not include an explicit privacy clause; moreover, Art. 27 emphasizes that individual rights and freedoms must be "exercised with due regard to...collective security, morality and common interest." There is no Asian regional human rights treaty.

accessible and which contains foreseeable standards as opposed to administrative policy or individual discretion not based on legal rules." The law must be shown to be strictly required to serve a legitimate purpose of society for which there is a pressing need. And finally, the measures adopted must be the least intrusive and strictly proportional to the urgent purpose they are designed to serve.[184] Mandatory testing of the Burmese women and girls for HIV/AIDS fails to meet any of these conditions.

To begin with, Thai law does not authorize mandatory testing of prostitutes. In 1991, AIDS was purposefully dropped from the list of notifiable diseases in the Infectious Diseases Act of 1980, which authorizes public health officials to take draconian measures to control the listed diseases.[185] Additionally, the Thai AIDS Plan explicitly rules out compulsory testing under any circumstances unless informed consent is given by the individual concerned or by her/his legal representative. The only exception are military and police officials who have to enter into combat situations or confront dangerous persons.[186]

Mandatory testing is neither strictly required nor effective. Public health experts appear to have reached a consensus that mandatory HIV screening is not an effective means for slowing the spread of this infection.[187] For the Burmese in brothels, knowledge of their HIV status has no remedial value as long as they are living under conditions that amount to slavery. The most effective way for the Thai government to protect these girls from HIV acquired through forced prostitution is to secure their release from the brothels and ensure their safe passage home.

By opting to test on a compulsory basis all the Burmese who were "rescued" and placed in Pakkret and some of those in brothels, the Thai government has selected one of the most intrusive and least effective measures for AIDS control. Prosecution of specific traffickers,

---

[184] UN Center for Human Rights and WHO, *AIDS and Human Rights*, p.15.

[185] Vitit Muntarbhorn, *HIV/AIDS, Ethics and the Law: The Case of Thailand*, May 1993, p.3-6 (draft).

[186] *Thailand's National AIDS Prevention Plan*, p.23.

[187] UN Center for Human Rights and WHO, *AIDS and Human Rights*, p. 42.

brothel owners, collaborators and customers would be more effective, as would public education (which does not depend on knowing the target audience's HIV status). Thus far, government-sponsored AIDS information campaigns have completely bypassed the Burmese and other foreigners.

HIV testing is an extension of an earlier system, predating the AIDS pandemic, that was created by the Ministry of Public Health to monitor Thai prostitutes. Provincial health officers were to test Thai women working in "entertainment places" about every three months for sexually-transmitted diseases.[188]   With the onset of the AIDS pandemic, HIV testing was added in 1989; the women and girls reportedly are not allowed to refuse the test and must show their health card in order to work in these registered places.

HIV testing was later rescinded through the 1992-1996 National AIDS Plan which, on paper, embodies greater human rights protections. However, due to inadequate monitoring, mandatory testing continues in ways that violate not only the right to informed consent, but also patients' medical confidentiality and right to know their own health status.

The health card system was originally limited to Thai women in registered "entertainment places." But it appears that, over time, some local officials have expanded the system at their own initiative to include some Burmese prostitutes in illegal brothels. Despite the official termination of the entire health card system in September 1992, there are credible reports that health cards continue to be used at the local level.[189]   Some of the Burmese we interviewed in January 1993 referred to their cards.

Testing in the brothels

As noted above, the Thai government policy banned mandatory testing in the 1992-1996 National AIDS Plan, which introduced guidelines for safeguarding human rights, including a ban on compulsory testing, a requirement of pre- and post-test counselling, and strict confidentiality of

---

[188] Although both prostitution and trafficking are illegal under Thai law, health monitoring of sex workers by the government was an implicit acknowledgement that the law against prostitution is hardly effective.

[189] Interview with a Thai NGO, July 29, 1993.

medical records.[190]   But because monitoring is inadequate, forced testing of women and girls in brothels without their informed consent continues to depend on the inclinations of local authorities and brothel owners. Some of the women and girls we interviewed did not know why their blood was extracted, and only realized after they were lectured about AIDS at Pakkret that they had been tested for HIV at the brothels.

> ● The operator of the brothel where "Nu Nu" worked took her to the doctor. She did not know who paid the medical bill, but she had to pay for her own medicine. She had a pink health card from the clinic she visited and the doctor tested her blood, but she was never told her results or what kind of medicine she was given. The doctor gave her health card directly to the brothel owner. She never had access to her own health records let alone the opportunity or ability to get them translated. She knew of AIDS from television. She thinks she contracted syphilis once, but she does not know if she has AIDS.

> ● "Nyi Nyi" (one of the women described in Chapter II) was tested for AIDS once in the teashop-cum-brothel and once in Pakkret. She was never told the results. She only knew at the time we interviewed her that she used to weigh fifty kilograms and now she weighed thirty-six kilograms. She was often sick but only learned about AIDS at Pakkret. She was afraid of the doctor and injections.

> ● "Thazin" was tested for AIDS four times in the brothel, but she had not known anything about AIDS before she got to Pakkret. They never told her the results of her test. She had never been to the doctor before [arriving in Thailand].

---

[190] *Thailand's National AIDS Prevention Plan*, p. 23.

Testing in official custody

The majority of Burmese girls and women who are "rescued" from the brothels by Thai officials are sent directly to local police stations. While twenty-four of the thirty Burmese women and girls we interviewed were later sent from the local police station to Pakkret and two directly to emergency shelters, this does not reflect the general trend. The majority of Burmese women and girls are arrested as illegal immigrants and sent to an immigration detention center (IDC). At the IDC no routine health care is provided, and girls and women are only allowed to receive medical care when they can show visible signs of a serious health emergency. These is no routine testing or treatment for STDs nor the HIV virus. However, when girls and women are sent for emergency health services, it has become routine practice to test for the HIV virus without informing the patient, requesting their consent or informing them of the results.

As noted above, approximately 150 Burmese women and girls who were "rescued" from the Thai brothels by the central Crime Suppression Division, largely during the government crackdown on forced prostitution during June and July 1992, were sent to Pakkret reformatory as part of an official repatriation. They were systematically tested there by public health personnel, even though this is not recommended by the National AIDS Prevention Plan, much less legally codified. They were mandatorily tested and although they received AIDS information, the testing was done without pre- and post-test counselling, and usually without being told their test outcomes.

● "Nu Nu" had her blood tested three times at Pakkret without being informed of the results, but she, along with other girls there, were told a lot about AIDS. She does not know what will happen to her once she is deported back to Burma.

● "Tar Tar" was tested for AIDS in Pakkret. The matrons told them they were all HIV positive and to use condoms with anyone they loved. She did not know if it was true or if the matrons at Pakkret were just trying to scare them.

- "Thazin" was also tested at Pakkret and again at an NGO shelter in Chiangmai, but was never given the results.

Testing at the Temporary Shelters

Several hundred of the Burmese women and girls who are "rescued" from the brothels have been placed under the temporary care of nongovernment emergency shelters. While receiving medical care, they are also tested for HIV at these shelters. From the perspective of the NGO shelter staff, testing is needed because the girls are living in close quarters and the "house parents" should know their HIV status in order to take the proper precautions.

No Voluntary Informed Consent

Mandatory testing is conducted without informed consent. Eleven of the thirty women and girls we interviewed reported having been required by the brothel owners to undergo screening at least once, either at the brothel or at a clinic. All nineteen who were sent through Pakkret said that they were tested while detained there.

- "Aye Aye," aged nineteen, who was sold to an agent at the age of fourteen, said that the brothel owner took her and other girls to be tested. He never told her the results, but she never got sick. She was also tested at Pakkret.

- "Nwe Nwe," a fourteen-year-old, said a doctor took her blood every week at the brothel, and she was also tested at Pakkret without being told the results.

- "Chit Chit" was tested four times in the first brothel in Chiangmai where she worked. Then she was tested twice while in another brothel in Bangkok. After her arrest by plainclothes policemen, she was tested again in Pakkret. She was never given the results from any of the tests.

- "Tar Tar" was tested for AIDS three times in the

brothels (twice in the Hotel See Tong brothel and once in Dao Kanong brothel). After her blood was taken she never saw the doctors again and never heard the results.

Breach of Medical Confidentiality

After being forcibly tested, the Burmese women and girls are routinely subjected to the further indignity of having their own test results withheld from them, even when they are aware that they have been tested for HIV and request to know their status. Knowledge of one's HIV status may be expected to enhance personal responsibility on the part of the Burmese women and girls, if not in the brothels where there is no freedom of choice, then after her escape or release from the brothels.

The testimony of "Tar Tar" and others described above is echoed by many others. All the Burmese women and girls we interviewed had been tested for HIV by, or at the behest of, the brothel owner, Pakkret reform house staff or the personnel at one of the emergency shelters. In all thirty cases, the women and girls themselves were never informed of their official test results. As a result, some may have received inaccurate unofficial information. For example, one girl was given her status off-handedly while her blood was being drawn in the brothel, but before the serum sample was even analyzed. Another learned of her status through a rumor circulated by non-medical staff at Pakkret. At least one girl was told casually that she was HIV negative when, in fact, according to an NGO, her health card indicated that she was positive.

Although the results were withheld from the women and girls, public health staff and at times, government officials, had the medical records. While there is no substantive Thai law on privacy, health professionals can be held criminally liable under the Thai Penal Code for breaching patient confidentiality. Section 323 of the Penal Code states:

> Whoever discloses any private secret which became known or communicated to him by reason of his functions as a competent official or his profession as a medical practitioner shall be punished with imprisonment not exceeding six months, or fine not exceeding one

thousand baht, or both.[191]

Moreover, both internationally-accepted guidelines as well as the National AIDS Plan emphasizes confidentiality as an imperative ethical norm in dealing with HIV/AIDS. According to the U.N. Centre for Human Rights and WHO, "a policy permitting or requiring the disclosure of the results of HIV tests to third persons without consent...amounts to an interference with privacy."[192] The Thai National AIDS Prevention Plan contains a similar injunction against revealing HIV status without the full and explicit consent of the infected person.[193]

In flagrant violation of these legal and ethical standards, Thai health officials fail to hold the HIV test results of the Burmese in the strictest confidence. Rather, they occasionally share them with people who have no medical reason to know. It is particularly reprehensible that brothel owners, who have repeatedly demonstrated their callous disregard for the women and girls' health, are sometimes given the test results of the Burmese under their control.[194]

Under the health card system, the HIV test results of women in registered "entertainment places" were required to be recorded on individual color-coded cards: pink if HIV negative, brown if positive. "HIV" (along with other STDs) are also stamped in large letters on these cards, which are accessible to brothel owners, health personnel, customers, and others. In the case of Thai prostitutes, brothel owners have exploited their knowledge of the women's HIV status in one of two ways: to maximize profit from "clean girls" by charging higher prices for them, or to expel those found to be infected.

---

[191] Muntarbhorn, *HIV/AIDS, Ethics and the Law*, p.11 (draft). In practice, however, this provision has rarely been invoked in Thai courts. The reasons include a strong cultural deference to doctors and fear of revealing one's health condition publicly.

[192] "International Consultation," p. 44.

[193] *Thailand's National AIDS Plan*, p. 23.

[194] For example, brothel owners use their knowledge of Thai prostitutes' HIV status in one of two ways: To maximize profit from "clean girls" by charging higher prices for them, or to expel those found to be infected.

The health card system, which continues in some places despite its official cancellation in November 1992, also invites abuses because few health officials take it seriously as an effective weapon against AIDS. So they either do not vigorously enforce mandatory testing, or are easily bribed into ignoring it. Brothel owners rarely have trouble negotiating a certificate of good health. Some even "have fun with pink cards" by arranging to have them arbitrarily stamped every week or month to "verify" that the girls are "clean."[195]It is a criminal offense under Thai law to falsify official documents when such an act is likely to have harmful consequences.[196] In practice, the customers rarely ask to see the cards. But when they do, the girls or brothel operators can show any card they want. In some of the more restrictive brothels, if a girl tests positive she continues to work but is simply no longer sent for screening.[197]

At the time of our research, Burmese women and girls who were placed under the care of temporary shelters after being "rescued" also were not told their test results by the staff of the NGOs. This has been a difficult decision for the NGOs to reach, and was made primarily because they feel that there is very little that either they or the Burmese girls can do with the information after repatriation.

Condoms were illegal in Burma until the end of 1992.[198] Health services in Burma are believed to be rudimentary, and Thai NGOs are well aware of reports of discrimination against and abuse of HIV positive persons in Burma. Those NGOs have no resources to hire and train Burmese interpreters and staff in AIDS intervention and counselling.

These concerns must be weighed against the merits of disclosure. In addition to respecting the Burmese women and girls' right to know their own test results, policymakers should fully consider the roles that women and girls working as prostitutes have beyond the brothel. At the 1989 International Conference on the Implications of AIDS for Mothers

---

[195] Interview with a Thai NGO, January 20, 1993.

[196] Thai Penal Code, Section 64.

[197] Interview with ACCESS, February 4, 1993.

[198] "Burma Slow to Face AIDS Crisis," *Washington Post*, April 1, 1993.

and Children, the assembled ministers of health stressed the importance
of ensuring "that *all* HIV infected women receive appropriate
information...so that they can personally make informed decisions about
child-bearing".[199] According to one doctor, "full disclosure -- ideally
with Western blot confirmation -- permits self-protection, the protection
of others, and the possibility of treatment should future therapeutic
breakthroughs occur."[200]

Discrimination

Mandatory testing also amounts to *de facto* discrimination against
prostitutes.[201] Individual doctors may have different reasons for
conducting mandatory testing, but the official policy, which has its origins
in the STD/HIV screening system, is primarily intended to make female
prostitutes safe for their clients.

According to Dr. Saisuree, the health certificates placed all the
burden on prostitutes to look after their health and made male customers
complacent about the need to protect themselves from contracting
AIDS.[202] This is most clearly illustrated by HIV testing at Pakkret.
Against all established international and national guidelines, female
prostitutes who are sent there are systematically tested, often repeatedly.

---

[199] Emphasis added. Paris Declaration on the Implications of AIDS for
Mothers and Children," Art. 8, November 27-30, 1989. The importance of this
declaration was stressed by the 43rd World Health Assembly in its resolution
WHA43.10.

[200] Michele Barry, M.D., "Ethical Considerations of Human Investigation In
Developing Countries: The AIDS Dilemma," *The New England Journal of Medicine*,
Vol. 319, No. 16 at 1084. ELISA, or enzyme-linked immunosorbent assay, and
Western blot are two tests for detecting the presence of antibodies in blood serum
(or other bodily fluid) to the AIDS virus. The ELISA test is less accurate than the
Western blot test, insofar as the former has a higher probability of yielding a
"false positive," or identifying a person as infected when in fact she is not.

[201] The only segment of the male population that is tested on a mandatory
basis is male military recruits. *AIDS in the World*, Appendix 8.2.

[202] "Saisuree: End Health Cards For Call Girls," *The Nation*, February 23,
1993.

Yet, the customers, pimps and brothel owners associated with the brothel from which the women are "rescued" are not subjected to mandatory screening, even though male-to-female transmission of HIV is at least three times as efficient as female-to-male transmission.[203] We do not argue that the men should be tested without voluntary informed consent, but rather that all testing that does not conform to WHO guidelines, and that only targets certain populations, must stop immediately.

The different medical confidentiality standards that apply to prostitutes versus men at STD clinics who are selected for national sentinel surveillance also have a disparate impact on women, who are the overwhelming majority of prostitutes. Under the National AIDS Plan, men who attend STD clinics are tested on an unlinked anonymous basis, providing the highest assurance of confidentiality. In contrast, prostitutes, in theory, are tested on a voluntary confidential basis.[204] In practice, they are not guaranteed even this much.

The health card system, too, mirrors the government's discriminatory tendency to blame prostitutes for infecting their customers. Thai prostitutes who test positive are supposed to be encouraged to abandon the sex industry and be escorted back to their home village by the police.[205] Even though the customers are participating in a business euphemistically called "entertainment," Thai authorities apparently believe that they deserve to be protected at government expense from further risk of infection. By contrast, no HIV/AIDS care or alternative employment opportunities are guaranteed by the government to the women who are returned home.

---

[203] The transmission probabilities are those used by the World Bank. Cited in *AIDS in the World*, Jonathan Mann et al., Eds., Harvard University Press, Cambridge, 1992, Appendix 6.1A.

[204] In unlinked anonymous testing, the blood or saliva sample is identified by a number or other code rather than by the name of the patient, since laboratories are only interested in aggregate statistics on HIV prevalence. Each sample cannot be traced to the patient. In voluntary confidential testing, the names of sources of blood or saliva sample for HIV testing are recorded and can be traced, but this information is supposed to be held in strict confidence by medical staff.

[205] Interview with ACCESS, July 28, 1993.

The above violations fly in the face of a growing international consensus among many public health experts that the public health and human rights interests are mutually reinforcing in the fight against AIDS worldwide.[206]   Respect for the human rights of people with HIV or AIDS contributes to the achievement of public health objectives -- limiting the spread of HIV, treating those with HIV or AIDS, and finding a cure -- by creating a safe climate for people to seek medical counselling and voluntary testing.

Conversely, mandatory testing drives people who may be infected and most in need of counselling underground, away from health care providers. Moreover, mandatory testing instills a false sense of security by giving the misguided impression that all those infected can be identified, and that everyone else is safe.[207]   If this leads to a relaxation of personal vigilance against infection, the spread of HIV/AIDS may be accelerated.

D. WITHHOLDING INFORMATION ABOUT HIV/AIDS

Despite the central government's official position of greater openness in acknowledging and addressing the AIDS pandemic through mass media campaigns in the last few years, foreigners from neighboring countries -- a majority of whom are Burmese -- have not been a target audience.

While the Burmese women and girls in the closed brothels are trapped in virtual slavery, unable to negotiate any aspect of their situation or count on police protection, information on AIDS is admittedly of limited practical use. Nonetheless, it is one of their only remaining lines of defense against contracting and transmitting the AIDS

---

[206] See, for example, Dr. Jonathan Mann, "AIDS: Discrimination and Public Health," paper presented to the Fourth International Conference on AIDS, June 1988.

[207] In actuality, test results are not always accurate. There is always a possibility of getting a false positive, even with the Western Blot test, the most accurate and expensive test currently available. On the other hand, a negative result does not mean one is not infected because there is a lengthy "window period" between infection and when the antibodies to the virus can be detected.

virus. AIDS education for the Burmese will help them assert some control over their lives by informing their decisions about marriage and children when they are eventually repatriated to their home villages. And information for the general public, including potential male customers, may hopefully deter some from high-risk behavior. Both the World Health Organization's Global Program on AIDS and the Thai National AIDS Prevention Plan lists public information and education as critical elements of the fight against AIDS.[208]

The Thai government has thus far failed to summon the necessary political will and financial resources to reach Burmese women and girls in closed brothels. Brothel operators are allowed to dictate the terms of access for health educators. At the same time, the language barrier remains a major obstacle: most Burmese women and girls do not speak or read Thai; many are illiterate even in Burmese. There are no official educational materials in the Burmese language, whether written pamphlets or public service announcements for television or radio, the latter two being the most common sources of information for our interviewees.

Our findings indicate that only a small percentage of the Burmese women and girls have any knowledge about HIV/AIDS. They are the approximately two hundred who were sent through Pakkret between June and August 1992. One interviewee, "Nilar", who worked in a Bangkok brothel for seven months, said, "the girls talked about it [AIDS] at the brothel, but it was like a rumor." It was not until "Nilar" was placed in Pakkret that she was told how serious AIDS is, saw pictures and got a full explanation. Most of the Burmese women and girls who have been routinely charged as illegal immigrants and jailed in immigration detention centers reported not knowing anything about HIV/AIDS except for rumors or radio spots all in Thai which they do not fully understand.

An independent 1992 study by Hnin Hnin Pyne revealed many

---

[208] WHO-GPA has noted that "the keystone of HIV prevention is information and education, as HIV transmission can be prevented through informed and responsible behavior." "Report of an International Consultation on AIDS and Human Rights," United Nations Centre for Human Rights and the World Health Organization's Global Program on AIDS, Geneva, 26-28 July 1989, p. 33. *Thailand's 1992-1996 National AIDS Prevention Plan* devotes a chapter to a public information plan, p. 8-14.

misconceptions about HIV/AIDS among Burmese prostitutes in Ranong:

> ● One group of women explained that the virus has little
> horns and is very "quick" and "strong." Another added
> that it cannot even be killed in boiling water...Some
> women believed they are protected from the virus,
> because they receive "injections" every three months.
> This is not unusual since it is a common belief among
> most Burmese villagers that a "shot in the arm" is a cure
> all.[209]

The Thai government's record in educating the Thai public about AIDS is considerably better. Even so, local officials in some areas have suppressed attempts by public health personnel to disseminate AIDS information.

Given the extreme rates of HIV infection among Burmese women and girls forced into prostitution, and Thai police complicity in protecting the trafficking rings, the Burmese deserve far more public health attention from the Thai government than they currently receive.

E. TREATMENT ON RETURN TO BURMA

The ordeal of the Burmese women and girls continues on the Burmese side of the border. In addition to fears of punishment by SLORC for unauthorized emigration and involvement in prostitution, both of which are prohibited under Burmese law, the returnees also have reason to be concerned about persecution against persons with HIV or AIDS. According to a report by the Burmese Department of Health in collaboration with WHO, UNDP and UNICEF, some population groups in Burma are tested on a mandatory basis, including "Myanmar [Burmese] citizens returning from abroad..." The report concludes:

> Not only are these practices not in accordance with
> individual rights and WHO regulations to which the
> Government of Myanmar [Burma] has subscribed, but
> they are also detrimental to the [AIDS] Program efforts

---

[209] Pyne, *AIDS and Prostitution in Thailand*, p.29-30. The "shots in the arms" are usually injectable contraceptives arranged by the brothel owners.

to limit the spread of HIV among the Myanmar population... The Review would like to stress that there is no technically justifiable reason for mandatory testing (except for blood donations) nor for active case finding of HIV infected persons.[210]

Among its recommendations for implementation of Burma's sentinel surveillance program, the Review Team stressed that "case finding is only justified for diagnostic purposes, or on request by the individual itself, provided that strict confidentiality or anonymity are guaranteed."[211]

The group of ninety-five Burmese women and girls who were deported under the official bilateral agreement on September 15, 1992 were mandatorily tested for the AIDS virus by SLORC officials after their arrival in Burma. As noted above, thirty-two women (and one baby) were found to be HIV positive. These women were given a special lecture and told to return every month, even though some came from poor families living far away from the academy. On November 19, 1993, Burmese Deputy Foreign Minister U Nyunt Swe claimed that fifty-two women who were uninfected had been returned home. The rest remained at the Police Academy for unspecified medical treatment. We learned in September 1993 that all were subsequently released.

---

[210] "A Joint Review of Myanmar's Medium Term Plan for the Prevention and Control of AIDS," Myanmar's Department of Health in collaboration with WHO, UNDP and UNICEF, October 12-16, 1992, p. 4.

[211] Ibid, p. 22.

VIII. INTERNATIONAL RESPONSE

U.S. POLICY AND TRAFFICKING

As noted in Chapter II, the U.S. use of Thailand as a rest and recreation center during the Vietnam War contributed directly to the growth in prostitution; the U.S. thus has a particularly responsibility to address the problem.   In recent years, the U.S. State Department's *Country Reports on Human Rights Practices* have described prostitution as one of Thailand's "most troubling social problems."[212]   Beginning in 1991, these *Country Reports* also recognized the problem of the "trafficking in women from hilltribe minorities and neighboring countries" and called it a "disturbing recent trend" that is reportedly favored by Thai brothel operators because such women "may be obtained more cheaply and their inability to speak Thai makes them easier to control."[213]

However, the *Country Reports* consistently fail to identify the role of state agents, in particular, members of the police, military and border patrols, in perpetuating the traffic in persons, as detailed in this report. The only case of official complicity ever mentioned in the *Country Reports* was a February 1991 incident in which the police arrested and charged fifteen employees of the state-owned Thai Airways International with involvement in the traffic in women.

To our knowledge, until this year, the U.S. has not made either the traffic in women and girls or forced prostitution in Thailand an issue in decisions regarding official aid to Thailand.   In contrast to the $4 million allocated by the U.S. in fiscal year 1993 to Thailand to control the traffic in narcotics, no U.S. aid is targeted to stop the traffic in women and girls. The U.S. Agency for International Development's Thailand mission has no program that specifically assists victims of sex trafficking or forced prostitution. However, in the language accompanying the draft

---

[212] US Department of State, *Country Reports on Human Rights Practices*, 1990, 1991, 1992.

[213] *Country Reports*, 1991, p. 1008.

148

1994 Foreign Appropriations Bill,[214] the U.S. Congress for the first time called upon the Thai government to prosecute all those responsible for trafficking and forced prostitution.

OTHER COUNTRIES

European institutions have expressed concern in various fora about the trafficking of Burmese women. The European Parliament, for example, passed a resolution on October 28, 1992, calling on member states of the European Community to "ensure that the authorities in Thailand make an effort to effectively suppress the trade in human beings" and to "take practical steps to end the scandal of sex tourism." It also called on the European Community to make resources available for "the creation and maintenance of women's homes to provide a refuge for the women affected" and for training and employment programs for Burmese women. The resolution was adopted a month after the official repatriation of the 95 Burmese women from Pakkret and also called on SLORC to investigate the fate of the deported women and girls.

Various international organizations have been formed to address the trafficking issue. In April 1993, ninety-four delegates from 17 Asian countries came together at a conference organized by the Coalition Against the Traffic of Women "to heighten awareness of the sex trade and to stem the sale of humans into bondage."[215] The issue of Burmese women sold into Thai brothels was highlighted.

The problem with expressions of concern and non-binding language and resolutions, however, is that they exert no real pressure on the governments of either Thailand or Burma to make real reforms.

HIV AND AIDS

If international efforts to stop the trafficking has been almost non-existent, there has been more international attention to the spread

---

[214] If approved by Congress, foreign assistance to Thailand in 1994 could amount to $1.8 million and $13.3 million in security and economic assistance, respectively. Department of State and Defense Security Assistance Agency, *Congressional Presentation for Security Assistance Program, Fiscal Year 1994*, p. 329.

[215] "17 Countries Meet to Combat Sex Slavery", *Chicago Tribune*, April 5, 1993.

of AIDS in Southeast Asia. Although U.S. development assistance to Thailand, for example, does not focus on the needs of women and girls in prostitution, the U.S. supports Thailand's AIDS prevention program, which heavily targets the sex industry. U.S. assistance to Thailand to combat the HIV/AIDS pandemic is administered by the U.S. Agency for International Development (USAID). The effectiveness of USAID's global HIV/AIDS initiative has been heavily criticized by the U.S. Government Accounting Office (GAO). In a report released in June 1992, the GAO noted that USAID's official policy guidance calls on USAID missions to make minimal efforts in the area of HIV/AIDS prevention, citing limited resources and the political sensitivity associated with this disease as justifications. Despite acknowledgement by USAID's top management that many aspects of the policy guidance is outdated, the USAID had not yet revised it.[216] The GAO study, which did not provide country-specific evaluations, concluded that "AID has not effectively addressed the serious implications of the spread of the virus in developing countries."[217]

In Thailand, prior to 1991, USAID collaborated mainly with nongovernment organizations while supplying condoms through the Thai government. USAID suspended assistance to Thailand in response to the 1991 Thai military coup and did not resume support until after a new civilian Thai government was elected in September 1992. Since then, approximately $2 million has been allocated to USAID's Thailand mission for a five-year period to combat HIV/AIDS. In addition, USAID is providing $8 million in central funding to the Thai National AIDS Prevention and Control Plan (AIDSCAP)[218] over the next five years. However, thus far, the implementation of this plan has not only largely failed to protect Burmese women and girls in Thai brothels from HIV infection, but has to some extent contributed to additional abuses against them. (See Chapter VII).

---

[216] US General Accounting Office, *Combating HIV/AIDS in Developing Countries*, June 1992, p. 15.

[217] *Ibid*, p. 21.

[218] AIDSCAP focuses on facilitating policy dialogues and institution building, rather than direct interventions.

UNITED NATIONS AGENCIES

Several U.N. organizations have offices in Rangoon, including the United Nations Development Program (UNDP); the United Nations Children's Fund (UNICEF); the World Health Organization (WHO); and the U.N. Drug Control Program (UNDCP). The U.N. High Commissioner on Refugees (UNHCR) is also setting up operations in Burma. Of these, UNDP has by far the largest budget, but all have the potential to address some aspects of trafficking.

WHO, for example, has a representative in Rangoon overseeing its activities and coordinating its work with Burmese health officials. Its proposed budget for 1994-95 is $7 million, covering a wide range of programs, including HIV prevention.

UNICEF carries out more than a dozen projects in Burma dealing with health and nutrition, education and early child development, water and sanitation, and other areas affecting mothers and children. The approved budget for 1991-95 is $40 million, but as of July 1993, only $7.3 million of this budget had been funded.

The largest and most visible program has been UNDP's. At the June 9, 1993 meeting of the UNDP Governing Council in New York, $18 million was approved for Burma programs through December 1994. Priorities include poverty alleviation, natural resource development, and HIV programs organized with WHO. All projects are supposed to be aimed at assisting sustainable development at the grassroots, community level.[219]

To our knowledge, however, none of these programs specifically address the relationship between trafficking and HIV/AIDS, since the U.N. agencies, by virtue of having to go through SLORC, have effectively restricted themselves from operating in the areas from which most of the trafficking victims come.

---

[219] This represents a major shift in UNDP's approach, following the call of some government representatives, including the United States, for a dramatic change how UNDP programs were structured. Referring to the "deplorable human rights situation," the U.S. said that it would not support infrastructure development projects and sectoral reform which would enhance SLORC's legitimacy.

IX. CONCLUSIONS AND RECOMMENDATIONS

Burmese women and girls lured into Thailand for the purposes of prostitution face a wide range of violations of international human rights law:

- they are trafficked into Thailand, often with the direct complicity of Thai police and other officials, in violation of the U.N. Convention on the Suppression of Traffic in Persons, the Convention on the Elimination of All Forms of Discrimination Against Women, customary international law, and, in the case of girls below the age of 18, the Convention on the Rights of the Child.
- they are forced to work as bonded labor and in conditions tantamount to slavery, in violation of the International Covenant on Civil and Political Rights, the Slavery Convention and the Supplementary Convention on the Abolition of Slavery, numerous ILO Conventions and customary international law.
- they are effectively deprived of their liberty in the brothels.
- when the brothels are raided by police, they are subjected to arbitrary and wrongful arrest and detention in immigration detention centers, and in some cases, penal reform institutions, in violation of international and national anti-trafficking norms and of the Body of Principles for the Protection of All Persons Under Any Form of Detention of Imprisonment.
- they face rape on arrival in Thailand but are not in a position and do not have the knowledge or means to bring charges against the perpetrators. Given police involvement in the brothels and that most of the victims are under 18, the fact that such abuse is routine is a clear violation of the obligation of the Thai government under the Convention on the Rights of the Child to "take all appropriate legislative, administrative, social and educational measures to protect the child from all forms of physical or mental violence, injury or abuse, neglect or negligent treatment, maltreat or exploitation, including sexual abuse."
- they are exposed to HIV by their clients in the brothel. That exposure is facilitated by their inability to choose clients or negotiate the terms of sex which in turn is a direct result of their status as bonded labor.
- they are then are tested for HIV without their knowledge or consent in violation not only of WHO guidelines but of the right,

152

guaranteed by the International Covenant on Civil and Political Rights, not to be subjected to arbitrary or unlawful interference with privacy. The fact that their clients are not similarly tested highlights the discriminatory nature of the testing.

● they face discrimination in the application of Thai domestic laws prohibiting prostitution, in violation of the Convention on the Elimination of All Forms of Discrimination Against Women.

● while in police custody, they are detained in conditions which fall far short of the U.N. Standard Minimum Rules for the Treatment of Prisoners and are subjected to sexual abuse and other forms of cruel and degrading treatment and custodial abuse.

● they are deported as illegal immigrants to face almost certain arrest on the Burmese side of the border for illegal departure, in violation of both the Convention on the Suppression of Traffic in Persons and the right, recognized in the International Covenant on Civil and Political Rights, to enter and leave one's own country.

These abuses are perpetuated by the failure of the Thai government to meet its obligations under international law and to enforce its own laws in an impartial and non-discriminatory manner. If there is a central theme running through this report, it is that the women and girls are punished, while the brothel owners, agents, pimps, clients and local officials involved in recruitment and brothel operations are not. The pattern of abuse can only be remedied if the governments of Thailand, Burma and the international community give the problem of trafficking the concerted attention it deserves.

RECOMMENDATIONS TO THE GOVERNMENT OF THAILAND

1. As a matter of urgency Thailand should accede to the two international instruments most relevant to the trafficking in women and girls: the International Covenant on Civil and Political Rights and the Convention for the Suppression of Traffic in Persons and the Exploitation of the Prostitution of Others.

2. The government of Thailand should move as quickly as possible to reform its prostitution and trafficking laws to, among other things, make them consistent with the Thai Penal Code; non-discriminatory; and in line with international human rights standards, particularly those designed to protect the victims of trafficking. While Human Rights Watch

takes no position on prostitution per se, we consider the exemption of clients from the Suppression of Prostitution Act to be discriminatory. If Thailand maintains the ban on prostitution, clients should also be penalized. At the same time, individuals forced into prostitution should be exempt from any punishment or involuntary remand to reform institutions.

3. As more and more official border crossings are opened between Burma and Thailand and roads are constructed linking the two countries, strict monitoring to guard against the trafficking in women and girls should be intensified, including the inspection of vehicles. Special training should be given to law enforcement officials at the border in the problem of trafficking and their obligation to protect trafficking victims and investigate those who engage in such abuse.

4. In accordance with Article 20 of the Convention on the Suppression of Traffic in Persons, the Thai government should monitor and investigate employment agencies or recruitment networks operating in known trafficking centers such as Mae Sot, Mae Sai and Ranong, "to prevent persons seeking employment, in particular women and children, from being exposed to the danger of prostitution."

5. The government of Thailand should actively investigate and prosecute all those involved in trafficking and brothel operations, with particular attention to its own police and officials who aid and abet the illegal entry of Burmese women and girls, receive pay offs or protection money from brothel owners and/or agents, patronize illegal brothels, have financial holdings in, collect rent from, or in any other way are complicit in the operations of such brothels.

Investigations of official involvement must be both thorough and impartial. A hotline, perhaps similar to the hotline established for disappearance victims following the May 1992 events in Bangkok, could be established to receive allegations of official involvement, with safeguards established for the protection of witnesses. Information could then be turned over to an commission of inquiry for investigation, with the record of the proceedings public to the extent that witness security permits. Prosecutions of officials, including members of the police and military, should take place in civilian courts in proceedings that are open to the public.

6. Officials found guilty of involvement in trafficking and/or brothel operations, or of failing to enforce the law with respect to those operations, should be prosecuted to the fullest extent of the law. Transfer to a different area, as was recommended for police officers in the Songkhla murder and more recently, for complicit law enforcement officials in general, is not sufficient.

7. All laws which can lead to the prosecution of all others involved in trafficking and brothel operations, including recruiters, agents, brothel owners and pimps, should be strictly enforced. Brothel owners, for example, are responsible for forcible procurement of women, outlawed under the Suppression of Prostitution Act, each time that they compel one of their workers to have sex with a client. Clients who engage in sex with children below the age of 15 could and should be arrested for rape under the Thai Penal Code.

8. The Thai government should cease immediately the practice of arresting trafficking victims. It is inconsistent with both national and international anti-trafficking norms and basic principles of due process. Instead, the government should work with local NGOs to devise suitable non-penal shelters for the women and girls pending their supervised repatriation to Burma, provided they have no well-founded fear of persecution. To the extent that Pakkret is seen as a prison and, in many cases, run as such, it does not constitute a non-penal alternative.

9. If the status of a woman or girl as a trafficking victim is not clear and she is arrested, the Thai government should ensure that her civil rights are fully protected, including that she understands the nature of the charges against her, has access to an interpreter and legal counsel and is tried without undue delay before a fair and impartial tribunal, with the right of appeal thereafter. In accordance with Thai law, no detainee should be held for longer than 48 hours without an order from a judge unless required by the needs of the investigation, in which case the detention can be extended to a week. Any case involving the detention of a Burmese woman or girl following a raid on a brothel should be given particular attention with a view toward the speedy release of anyone found to be a trafficking victim.

10. To protect Burmese women and girls against abuse in Thai police

lock-ups and immigration detention centers, the Thai government should ensure the presence of women police officers and guards responsible for women's sections of prisons. The government should also investigate any report of extortion and sexual abuse in the prison and prosecute those responsible to the fullest extent of the law. The rights of detainees to be protected against abuse and the procedures for submitting complaints against officials should be available in the Burmese language in Thai prisons and be explained fully to detainees on arrival.

11. The Thai government should ensure that the Immigration Detention Center in Bangkok, local immigration detention facilities, and local jails conform fully to the U.N. Standard Minimum Rules for the Treatment of Prisoners.

12. In keeping with the Convention on the Suppression of Traffic in Persons and improving on the model established with the official repatriation of ninety-five women from Pakkret in 1992, the Thai government should arrange with the Burmese government for the safe return of trafficking victims. In the case of indigent women, it should bear the cost of their repatriation to the border and arrange for Burma to bear any additional costs. The agreement with the Burmese government should contain guarantees that the women and girls will not be arrested, fined or in any way held accountable for illegal departure or prostitution. Under no circumstances should the Thai government agree to selective and discriminatory repatriation on the basis of the ethnic or racial background of the women and girls concerned.

13. Because of the danger that Burmese women and girls can be arrested upon return to Burma for having engaged in prostitution or having emigrated illegally, the Thai government should protect the women's right to privacy by prohibiting access to confidential or biographical information about the women. (The Thai press should also agree on an ethical code that would restrict the use of names or identifiable photographs of these women from appearing in the print or broadcast media unless the women in question have specifically consented.)

14. The Thai government should secure agreement from the Burmese government that Thai officials and/or appropriate international organizations will be able to monitor the safety and well-being of any

returnees. It should then follow through with visits within a few months of the repatriation and examine, through confidential interviews with the returnees, procedures in place on the Burmese side, including any interrogation, medical testing or subsequent surveillance.

15. The Thai government should put in place adequate asylum screening procedures, so that victims of trafficking who claimed to fear persecution if returned to Burma could be interviewed and their claims impartially assessed.

16. Until such time as official repatriations with adequate safeguards for the protection of Burmese women and girls become routine, any deportation of Burmese women and girls should take place only under the observation of officials from Bangkok or members of respected international organizations. Such observation is necessary to guard against the abuse described in this report whereby brothel agents await the arrival of deportation buses and recruit deportees back into the brothels, with the full knowledge and complicity of local Thai officials.

17. The Thai government should end discriminatory and compulsory HIV testing of prostitutes, and if testing of a non-compulsory nature, with the informed consent of the women and girls is undertaken, those tested should be informed of the results if they so request.

RECOMMENDATIONS TO THE GOVERNMENT OF BURMA

1. Burma, like Thailand, should ratify or accede to the key international instruments relevant to the trafficking in women and girls (In 1956, Burma signed but never ratified the Convention for the Suppression of Traffic in Persons and the Exploitation of the Prostitution of Others.) It should also bring domestic legislation and its own practices into conformity with international human rights norms. It is unrealistic to suppose that any advances in the protection of potential trafficking victims can be made without a more general improvement in the human rights situation, particularly in the area of freedom of expression and the ability to criticize individuals and policies. At the same time, no punishment of local officials complicit in trafficking is likely as long as impunity of SLORC officials for human rights offenses more generally remains unchallenged.

2. The State Law and Order Restoration Council (SLORC) should take an active role in monitoring and preventing the trafficking of Burmese citizens into Thailand. By means of radios, posters and other means, it should alert its citizens to the dangers of recruitment and trafficking, with particular attention to rural areas of Shan State and to Kawthaung. The AIDS epidemic should be specifically discussed in the context of trafficking.

3. Negotiations with Thailand to open border crossings should include establishing systems for monitoring the trafficking in women and girls, and investigating and prosecuting the traffickers to the fullest extent of the law.

4. SLORC should permit frequent and systematic monitoring of returned Burmese trafficking victims by Thai officials and international organizations to ensure the protection of the women and girls from further detention, harassment, abuse or discrimination. SLORC should also permit access by international human rights and humanitarian organizations to areas around the Thai and Chinese borders to investigate trafficking and related abuses.

5. No trafficking victims repatriated from Thailand or any other country should be subjected to arrest, imprisonment, surveillance or compulsory medical testing on return to Burma.

RECOMMENDATIONS TO THE INTERNATIONAL COMMUNITY

1. The Secretary-General of the United Nations, under the terms of a November 1993 General Assembly resolution on human rights in Burma[220] that calls on him to assist in the implementation of the resolution, should ensure that all United Nations agencies pay particular attention to the issue of trafficking in women and develop programs and strategies designed to curb that abuse. (The resolution specifically mentions abuse against women as one of the human rights violations of concern in Burma.) U.N. agencies such as UNICEF, WHO and UNDP, all of which have AIDS prevention programs in Burma, should be called

---

[220] Situation of Human Rights in Myanmar, United Nations General Assembly, A/C.3/48/L.70, 29 November 1993.

upon to investigate reports of discrimination against and persecution of people with HIV and those considered high risk for HIV, including most of the women and girls who return from Thailand.

2. Particularly since trafficking of women appears to be increasing throughout Asia and the governments of China, Malaysia and Indonesia, among others, have expressed concern about the fate of their citizens, the situation in Thailand offers an opportunity to develop a model for prevention of trafficking and protection of victims that may be applicable to other countries. Upcoming events that offer the possibility for expressions of concern and the development of regional strategies to address the problem are the June 1994 Asian regional preparatory meeting in Jakarta, Indonesia for the 1995 Beijing Women's Conference and the Association of Southeast Asian Nations (ASEAN) meeting in Bangkok shortly thereafter. At the latter meeting, the ASEAN governments will decide whether or not to grant Burma observer status in ASEAN.

3. Asian countries and donor countries outside the region should encourage Thailand and Burma to adopt the recommendations outlined above and should use every opportunity to raise the problem of trafficking both publicly, at international meetings, Congressional or parliamentary hearings, and in press conferences; and privately, in meetings with relevant officials. They should also work to develop programs and strategies for bilateral and multilateral aid programs to Thailand that would make funds available for certain kinds of training, education, information dissemination and legal reform programs related to trafficking, but would also make some assistance programs conditional on evidence of effective prosecution of officials, brothel owners, agents and pimps.

Donor countries should also take care to ensure that any loans financed through multilateral lending institutions for the construction of roads or other infrastructure projects near the Thai-Burmese border or the Sino-Burmese border include a system for monitoring the impact on trafficking in women, direct or indirect, that such a project would be likely to have. The potential problem should be raised with the countries involved and the loans be granted only on the condition that regular impact assessments be made.

4. Influential countries, such as Japan, which have good relations with both Thailand and Burma and which have ratified the relevant international instruments related to trafficking, should urge the latter two countries to ratify or accede to those instruments and to work out an agreement on repatriation and monitoring of trafficking victims.

5. Embassies of concerned governments in Thailand should ask to be kept informed of planned repatriations of Burmese women and girls and try to ensure that international observers are present. Likewise, embassies in Rangoon should quietly seek to monitor for themselves the well-being of returned women and girls.

6. The mandate of Professor Yozo Yokota, Special Rapporteur on Human Rights in Myanmar appointed by the United Nations Commission on Human Rights, should be expanded specifically to include attention to the recruitment of Burmese women and girls to work in Thai brothels and their situation after return to Burma.